Whither Religious

A survey of post-primary teachers in Ireland

by

John A. Weafer & Ann M. Hanley

with commentaries edited by

Dermot A. Lane

THE COLUMBA PRESS
DUBLIN 1991

First edition, 1991, published by
THE COLUMBA PRESS
93 The Rise, Mount Merrion, Blackrock, Co Dublin.

Cover by Bill Bolger
Originated by The Columba Press
Printed in Ireland by
Colour Books Ltd, Dublin

ISBN: 1 85607 039 5

TABLE OF CONTENTS

ACKNOWLEDGEMENTS

This Report is the result of the co-operation and initiative of a number of people who gave generously of their time in planning and completing the research. The project was initiated by the Catechetical Association of Ireland who, in conjunction with the Episcopal Commission for Catechetics, requested the Council for Research and Development to undertake the research. Our work was greatly facilitated by the assistance given by a number of representatives of these associations: Fr Pierce Murphy, Ms Phil Browne, Fr Paul Murphy, Sr Kathleen Glennon, Fr Pat Devitt, and Fr Dermot Lane.

We would also like to thank Bishops Murray, Finnegan, Kirby, and Lagan of the Episcopal Commission for Catechetics, and Bishops Kavanagh and Newman of the Council for Research and Development for their support and interest shown in the project. A special word of thanks is due to the Council's secretary, Ms Teresa Finegan, for typing the questionnaire and numerous drafts of the Report.

The late Dr Ann Breslin S.S.L., former Director of the Council for Research and Development, was responsible for the project's research design and initial development. Her expertise and commitment to the success of the project is gratefully acknowledged. May she rest in peace.

Finally, we are especially grateful to the 679 teachers who gave generously of their time and expert advice to complete a relatively long and detailed questionnaire. It is hoped that their generosity will be rewarded with the implementation of measures which will assist them in their work.

John A. Weafer (Director)
Ann M. Hanley (Research Assistant)

LIST OF TABLES

Table 4.2   Religious Education has a High Profile
               Among Administration, Staff, and Pupils
               by Selected Characteristics   68
Table 4.3   Ways in Which Religious Education could
               have a Higher Profile in the School   73
Table 4.4   Average Time Allocated Per Class to Junior and
               Senior Cycle Religious Education Each Week   73
Table 4.5   Number of Hours of Religious Education
               taught by Respondents Each Week
               – Junior and Senior Cycle   74
Table 4.6   Respondents are Satisfied that Religious
               Education has Sufficient Periods on the Junior
               and Senior Cycle Timetable   75
Table 4.7   Reasons for Dissatisfaction with Religious Education
               Timetabling for Junior Cycle   76
Table 4.8   Reasons for Dissatisfaction with Religious Education
               Timetabling for Senior Cycle   76
Table 4.9   Teachers Have An Opportunity to Discuss
               Their Subject with Other Religious Education
               Teachers   77
Table 4.10   Opportunities for Discussing Religious Education
               with Other Teachers   78
Table 4.11   Reasons Why Respondents have No Opportunities
               for Discussion with Other Religious Education
               Teachers   78
Table 4.12   Religious Education Teachers Talked to
               Individual Parents   79
Table 4.13   Occasions for Discussion of Religious Education
               with Parents of Pupils   79
Table 4.14   Respondents Found the Interchange With
               Parents Helpful   80
Table 4.15   Helpfulness of Principal, Chaplain, Diocesan
               Advisor to Religious Education Teachers   81

CHAPTER FIVE
Table 5.1   Religious Education is a Public Examination in
               Respondents' School in Northern Ireland   83
Table 5.2   Respondents are Satisfied with Arrangements
               Regarding the Public Examination of Religious
               Education in Junior Cycle   84
Table 5.3   Religious Education Should be a Leaving
               Certificate/G.C.S.E. Subject   85

Dedicated to the memory of Dr Ann Breslin SSL,
Director of the Council for Research and Development (1980-1988)
who died on March 23rd 1991

FOREWORD

It is a pleasure to welcome the publication of *Whither Religious Education? A Survey of Post-Primary Teachers in Ireland,* with commentaries.

Religion teachers, and indeed all Catholic teachers, play a most important role in the life of the Church:

"There is no more important apostolate than catechesis, the teaching of the faith. There is no greater and closer involvement of the laity in the life and mission of the Church than the involvement of Catholic teachers." (*Handing on the Faith* [1980])

This survey will, I hope, play an important part in increasing the sense of solidarity among Religion teachers and in building up their support for one another. It will also offer to other teachers, to parents, to clergy and to the whole community, a better understanding of the work of Religious Education in post-primary schools.

I thank John Weafer and the staff of the Research and Development Unit for their efficient work and their courteous co-operation. Gratitude is also due to everyone who took part so constructively and so generously in preparing, organising and responding to the survey, especially to schools, teachers and Diocesan Advisors. Excellent work has been done by many people in preparing the Survey for publication. In particular, I am grateful to Father Dermot Lane who gathered and edited the commentaries, and to those who willingly agreed to write them.

The Catechetical Association of Ireland, which originally suggested the undertaking and which provided a great deal of help at every stage, will have a large role in bringing the results to the attention of teachers, as well as in drawing the lessons and implementing the conclusions which will, I hope, emerge from the discussion of the results of the survey.

I hope that this survey will not only be of great help to Religous Educators, but that it will also enable the whole community of the Church to understand better and to support more effectively the work of teachers of Religion in the most important apostolate of catechesis.

✠ *Donal Murray*
Chairman, Episcopal Commission on Catechetics

Executive Summary

Section I: Introduction

This Report on the attitudes, ideals, needs and problems of Religious Education teachers at post-primary level in Ireland, presents the findings of a survey of 679 Religious Education teachers in the Republic of Ireland and Northern Ireland. While the principal focus of the survey was on evaluating the experiences of teaching Religious Education in different school environments, other topics included in the survey were: an evaluation of the texts and other resources used in teaching Religious Education; measuring the extent of collaboration which exists between Religious Education teachers and other people in related fields, such as school administrators, diocesan advisors, parish clergy and parents; the perceived status of Religious Education in schools; and the perceived need for additional support services for Religious Education teachers.

Section II: Study Background and Objectives

The survey, conducted in the months of April to June 1989, by the Irish Hierarchy's research unit, the Council for Research and Development, was commissioned by the Episcopal Commission for Catechetics and the Catechetical Association of Ireland. The principal reason for undertaking the survey was the recognition by the Commissioning Bodies of the need for a professional nationwide survey on the attitudes, needs and aspirations of Religious Education teachers in Ireland. Since most, if not all, of the larger surveys on Religion in Ireland conducted in recent years have focused on the general population or on specific age groups within this population, it is hoped that the results of this survey of Religious Education teachers will augment the findings of previous research.

Section III: The Sample of Teachers

The sample of teachers for this research project was drawn from Catholic post-primary schools in the Republic of Ireland and Northern Ireland by means of a stratified, multi-stage sampling procedure. A relatively large, comprehensive questionnaire was sent to 1,500 teachers throughout Ireland and 679 teachers replied. The youthfulness and strong lay representation among Religious Education teachers were particularly noticeable: approximately one-quarter (24%) of respondents were less than 31 years of age and the majority (61%) of respondents were lay persons. More than half (54%) of the respondents had formal Religious Education qualifications.

Section IV: Summary of Main Findings

This summary of the Report's main findings will be divided into the following sections:

(i)   Respondents' Experience of Teaching Religious Education
(ii)   Evaluation of Religious Education Texts
(iii) Perceived Status of Religious Education
(iv)   The Role of Religious Education in the Future

(i) Respondents' Experience of Teaching Religious Education

Most respondents were positive about their experiences as Religious Education teachers. The majority (60%) of teachers, particularly those with some Religious Education qualifications, felt the experience of teaching Religious Education was a rewarding experience, even if for most of them it was also quite challenging. However, a substantial minority (38%) of teachers perceived the experience of teaching Religious Education as difficult and almost one in ten of the total group usually found it a very difficult experience.

When asked if they found teaching Religious Education more or less satisfying than teaching other subjects, approximately equal percentages of respondents said they found Religious Education to be "more satisfying" (30%), "less satisfying" (32%) or "about the same" (35%). Respondents who perceived the experience as less satisfying comprised a higher proportion of males than females and more respondents without Religious Education qualifications than those with some formal training.

Most (52%) respondents continue to teach Religious Education because they have a personal interest in teaching this subject or a personal interest in teaching generally (20%). The perceived importance of teaching Religious Education for the majority of respondents was also evident in the proportion of respondents (63%) who had never seriously considered giving up teaching Religious Education.

In addition, the majority of teachers agreed with the suggestions that "a teacher's own faith is a vital component in fostering faith in the classroom" (95%) and that "religion is caught, not taught" (67%). In the latter case, however, a large number of teachers felt religion was both caught and taught.

When asked to evaluate the changes which have occurred in their teaching experience, the majority (59%) of teachers believed their experience of teaching Religious Education had changed "for better", compared with 16 per cent who considered the change had been "for worse", and 26 per cent who had "mixed" views on the matter.

Over half (53%) of the respondents found it difficult to teach some topics. This was particularly the case with theological subjects, sexuality and the sacraments.

(ii) Evaluation of Religious Education Texts

The majority (87%) of respondents use Religious Education texts regularly and most respondents were generally satisfied with the usefulness of these texts in teaching. In general, the characteristics of texts which appealed most to respondents were overall presentation, use of stories, inclusion of assignments and resource material, the use of illustrations, and real life examples. Conversely, those characteristics which were perceived as least useful by respondents included the use of difficult language and concepts, the advanced and abstract nature of the contents, the use of boring and irrelevant material, the absence of illustrations and the omission of ade quate details.

The *Christian Way Series* was used most often by respondents in the junior cycle, while the *Living Faith Series* was most popular in the senior cycle. While many teachers indicated general satisfaction with the *Christian Way Series*, most (88%) teachers felt they would like to see some changes if the series was presented again, particularly in its language and the need for additional contemporary material which would make the serious more relevant and attractive to students.

In addition to texts, most (98%) teachers used other resources in teaching. The three most popular resource materials used by respondents were discussion, the Bible, and prayer/meditation.

A substantial proportion (45%) of respondents felt topics were omitted from their course texts which they would like to see included. These topics included theology, social problems, spirituality, sexuality, other religions, personal development, sacraments and the Bible.

(iii) Perceived Status of Religious Education

The majority (69%) of respondents felt Religious Education had a high profile in the school among administration. In contrast, however, the status of Religious Education was perceived to be lower among staff members (42%), senior pupils (30%) and junior pupils (56%). When asked to suggest ways in which Religious Education might have a higher profile in the school, the three most frequently cited suggestions were, the need for more resources for Religious Education, changes in the Religious Education programme, and giving examination status to Religious Education.

The majority of respondents teach between one and four hours Religious Education each week. However, respondents with formal qualifications in Religious Education taught substantially more hours than their unqualified colleagues.

Most teachers considered the principal (87%), chaplain (79%) and diocesan advisor (81%) to be helpful to them in the course of their work as Religious Education teachers.

(iv) The Role of Religious Education in the Future
The majority of respondents in Northern Ireland said they were satisfied with arrangements for the public examination of Religious Education at junior cycle (81%) and also at senior cycle (80%).

Approximately half (51%) of all respondents were in favour of Religious Education being a Leaving Certificate/G.C.S.E. subject, compared with 24 per cent who were against the idea and 25 per cent who were unsure. Conversely, only one-third of respondents felt Religious Education should be an examination at junior certificate level.

Most (89%) respondents would like to see co-operation between their school and the wider parish in teaching Religious Education. However, in the case of respondents who had previously co-operated with the parish, approximately one-fifth were dissatisfied and just over one-quarter had mixed feelings about the experience.

Finally, a substantial number of teachers felt poorly prepared to teach Religous Education and would welcome inservice experiences and support services to assist them in their teaching.

Introduction

1.1 *Focus of Report*

This Report on the attitudes, ideals, needs and problems of Religious Education teachers at post-primary level in Ireland[1], presents the findings of a survey of 679 Religious Education teachers in the Republic of Ireland and Northern Ireland. While the principal focus of the survey was on evaluating the experiences of teaching Religious Education in different school environments, other topics included in the survey were: an evaluation of the texts and other resources used in teaching Religious Education; measuring the extent of collaboration which exists between Religious Education teachers and other people in related fields, such as school administrators, diocesan advisors, parish clergy and parents; the perceived status of Religious Education in schools; and the perceived need for additional support services for Religious Education teachers.

1.2 *Study Background and Objectives*

The survey, conducted in the months of April to June 1989, was commissioned by the Episcopal Commission for Catechetics and the Catechetical Association of Ireland. The principal reason for undertaking the survey was the recognition by the Commissioning Bodies of the need for a professional nationwide survey on the attitudes, needs and aspirations of Religious Education teachers in Ireland. Since most, if not all, of the larger surveys on Religion in Ireland[2] conducted in recent years have focused on the general population or on specific age groups within this population, it is hoped that the results of this survey of Religious Education teachers will augment the findings of previous research. The results of these latter surveys portray a picture of Irish youth as having weaker religious beliefs and lower levels of religious practice than their older counterparts. In addition, many young people would appear to be critical of certain aspects of the Church[3]. Although young people in Ireland are still very orthodox in religious beliefs and practice, especially when compared with Europe as a whole, the gradual movement away from traditional Church practices by an increasing number of young people suggests that comparable pressures would also be felt in areas which seek to teach

Religious Education and/or transmit the basics of the Catholic faith.
The absence of comprehensive information on this issue was one of
the principal motivating factors for undertaking this study. More specifically, the objectives of the survey were:

(a)   to document the attitudes, ideals and aspirations of a repre-
       sentative group of Religious Education teachers in Ireland;
(b)   to devise methods of assisting in the realisation of Religious
       Education teachers' ideals and aspirations;
(c)   to identify specific difficulties encountered by Religious
       Education teachers and to suggest possible remedies;
(d)   to examine the extent of, and highlight the need for, collabora-
       tion between Religious Education teachers and the following
       groups:
       - School Administrators
       - Diocesan Advisors
       - Parish Clergy and Parish Structures
       - Parents
(e)   to plan for the future development of training, support, and
       in-service facilities for Religious Education teachers, at local
       and national level, based on the results of this survey.

1.3   Research Strategy

The principal research strategy employed in this survey was a comprehensive postal questionnaire which was designed by the staff of
the Council for Research and Development in consultation with representatives of the Commissioning Bodies and 24 experienced Religious
Education teachers (Appendix III). This latter group of teachers were
asked to complete a draft version of the questionnaire and to offer relevant comments on any aspect of the questionnaire with which they
were not satisfied. The views of the 24 teachers who participated in
the pilot study were taken into account and, based on their recommendations, a number of changes were made to the draft questionnaire. Other suggestions were received from persons with a professional interest in Religious Education in Ireland. Accordingly, the final
version of the questionnaire which was sent to more than 1,500 teachers throughout Ireland represents the considered views of a relatively
large group of persons with experience of Religious Education teaching and training in Ireland.

In addition to the many statistically-based "quantitative" questions
which concentrated on numbers within each category, other questions
were included in the questionnaire which were more "qualitative".
The purpose of these latter questions was to provide respondents with

the scope to elaborate in their own words on any topic related to the teaching of Religious Education. The huge variety of answers received, although very time-consuming and difficult to group into general categories, nevertheless added significantly to the depth of the responses and ultimately, to the scope and richness of this Report.

1.3.2   Sample Design

The sample for this research project was drawn on the basis of a stratified, multi-stage sampling procedure. The initial step in this process entailed compiling a list of Catholic[4] post-primary schools in the Republic of Ireland and Northern Ireland. The distribution of these schools by location and school type is presented in Table 1.1.

Table 1.1   Distribution of Catholic Schools by School Type in the Republic of Ireland and Northern Ireland, 1988.

School Type	Number
Republic of Ireland	
Secondary Schools	479
V.E.C. Schools	253
Community Schools	45
Comprehensive Schools	11
Northern Ireland	
Grammar Schools	30
Maintained Schools	75
Total	893

Source: List of Post-Primary Schools 1987-1988, Stationery Office, Dublin; Department of Education, Northern Ireland.

The second stage in the selection process entailed compiling a list of all Religious Education teachers from approximately two-thirds of the schools. These schools were chosen by means of stratified random procedures, thereby preserving the statistically representative basis of the selection process.

In order to ensure that the selection of Religious Education teachers was representative of the various geographical areas in the country, the schools were selected from the four provinces according to population patterns.

The time-consuming task of compiling a comprehensive list of Religious Education teachers was carried out with the assistance of post-primary diocesan advisors and school principals. Lists of teachers involved in Religious Education were drawn up for each of the schools, indicating their gender, religious or lay status, as well as their qualifications and the class levels taught[5]. A random sample of 1,500 teachers was then selected from this list, taking into account their gender, Religious Education qualifications (if any), religious or lay status, and geographical background. A total of 1,200 teachers were selected in the Republic of Ireland and 300 in Northern Ireland. The questionnaires were posted to the 1,500 teachers selected with an accompanying explanatory letter from the Council's Director in April 1989 (Appendix II).

The initial response to the postal questionnaire (14%, N=216) was considered unsatisfactory and a reminder letter was sent in May 1989. The additional cost involved in posting this reminder letter was felt to be justified in the positive response rate it engendered. By the end of June 1989, 697 questionnaires had been returned. Of these, 18 were discarded as invalid, giving a final valid response rate of 45% (N=679).

1.4   Profile of Sample
This section of the chapter presents a profile of the 679 Religious Education teachers who replied to the questionnaire in terms of age, gender, status, experience, qualifications and geographical location. It also compares demographic characteristics of respondents in this sample with those of respondents in the national profile of Religious Education teachers (outlined in detail in Appendix I).

1.4.1   Gender and Age of Respondents
The majority (59%) of respondents in this study were female; 41% were male[6]. Respondents were quite evenly distributed across the age spectrum. A breakdown of the age structure of respondents in the sample is provided in Table 1.2.

Table 1.2   Age of Respondents

Age Group	Number	% of Total (N=659)*
20 - 30 years	158	24.0%
31 - 40 years	188	28.5%
41 - 50 years	184	27.9%
51 - 60 years	96	14.6%
61 years and over	33	5.0%
Total	659	100.0%

* 20 respondents did not indicate their age

Throughout the remainder of this Report, when age comparisons are made, the following categories will be used:

Less than 31 years	158	24.0%
31 - 40 years	188	28.5%
41 - 50 years	184	27.9%
More than 50 years	129	19.6%
Total	659	100.0%

1.4.2   Status of Respondents

The majority (61%) of respondents were lay persons; religious personnel accounted for the remaining 39%. The table below presents the distribution of respondents according to their status (i.e. lay, priest, religious brother, religious sister).

Table 1.3 Status of Respondents

Status	Number	% of Total (N=670*)
Lay Person	406	60.6%
Priest	73	10.9%
Religious Brother	37	5.5%
Religious Sister	154	23.0%
Total	670	100.0%

* Nine respondents did not indicate their status

On average, lay persons and priests were found to be younger than religious brothers and sisters. For example, 52% of lay persons and 36% of priests were aged 35 years or less, while only 3% of religious brothers and 8% of religious sisters fell into this age group.

1.4.3   Length of Religious Education Teaching Experience

Respondents were found to have varying amounts of Religious Education teaching experience. Table 1.4 overleaf details the duration of this experience.

Table 1.4 Length of Religious Education Teaching Experience

Duration	Number	% of Total (N=668*)
One year	38	5.7%
Two years	32	4.8%
Three years	41	6.1%
Four years	27	4.0%
Five years	36	5.4%
Six years	26	3.9%
Seven years	23	3.4%
Eight years	33	4.9%
Nine years	14	2.1%
Ten years	48	7.2%
11 - 15 years	130	19.5%
16 - 20 years	107	16.0%
21 - 30 years	79	11.8%
31 years and over	34	5.1%
Total	668	100.0%

* 11 respondents failed to answer this question

The six categories presented below will be employed throughout the remainder of this Report when describing length of Religious Education teaching experience.

Three years or less	111	16.6%
Four - seven years	112	16.7%
Eight - ten years	95	14.2%
11 - 15 years	130	19.5%
16 - 20 years	107	16.0%
21 years and over	113	16.9%
Total	668	100.0%

The majority of respondents stated that their careers as Religious Education teachers had been spent entirely in Ireland, only 14% had taught Religious Education in another country. Of those who had worked outside Ireland, the largest percentage (31%) had taught in England; 22% in Africa; 21.5% in North America; 11% in Australia; 7% in Europe; 5% in South America and 2% in Asia. One-fifth (20%) of those who had taught in a country other than Ireland had done so for one year or less; 43% for between two and five years; 37% for more than five years. Thirty-nine per cent of these had completed their teaching abroad between 1980 and 1989; 68% between 1970 and 1979; 24% prior to 1970.

1.4.4   Religious Education Qualifications

When asked to indicate whether or not they had received Formal Training for teaching Religious Education, the majority (82%) of respondents listed at least one qualification which they felt represented formal training. However, as the findings in Table 1.5 show, only 54% of respondents possessed formal qualifications. Details of respondents' highest[7] level of formal qualifications are outlined in Table 1.5 below.

Taking the top three categories listed in Table 1.5 as formal qualifications, this means that just over half (54%) of the respondents have a formal Religious Education qualification, compared with 46% who do not. However, it must be emphasised that this does not mean that almost half of the pupils are taught by unqualified teachers. Rather, the workload of teachers with specific catechetical qualifications tends to be considerably higher than their colleagues with no qualifications.

Table 1.5   Highest Formal Training in Religious Education

Formal Training	No.	% of Total (N=679)
Religious Education Degree/Diploma[8]	174	25.6%
Theology	101	14.9%
Teacher Training	89	13.1%
Religious Education Post-Graduate Diploma[9]	104	15.3%
Extra-mural Course	113	16.7%
None	98	14.3%
Total	679	100.0%

The relationship between Religious Education qualifications and number of hours taught is presented in Table 1.6 overleaf. The results in this table confirm the positive correlation between qualifications and hours taught. More than three-quarters (76%) of respondents with a "Religious Education Degree/Diploma", for instance, teach at least five hours per week at junior level, compared with less than one-fifth (19%) of respondents with no Religious Education or Theology qualifications. This same trend is also evident in the senior cycle.

Table 1.6   Hours Taught in Religious Education by Level of Qualification

Hours Taught	R.E. Degree or Diploma	Theology	Teacher Training	R.E. Post-grad.	Other None
JuniorCycle:					
1-2 hours	12.5%	20.0%	32.3%	30.7%	45.3%
3-4 hours	11.2%	24.0%	30.8%	29.3%	35.2%
5-10 hours	50.0%	34.7%	29.2%	26.7%	16.5%
11 hours+	26.3%	21.3%	7.7%	13.3%	2.9%
Subtotal	100.0%	100.0%	100.0%	100.0%	100.0%
SeniorCycle:					
1-2 hours	13.2%	23.5%	28.8%	33.3%	55.2%
3-4 hours	22.6%	30.9%	15.3%	39.7%	28.6%
5-10 hours	55.3%	32.1%	25.4%	21.8%	14.3%
11 hours+	8.8%	13.6%	30.5%	5.1%	1.9%
Subtotal	100.0%	100.0%	100.0%	100.0%	100.0%

A profile of respondents according to their qualifications and demographic characteristics is presented opposite.

Table 1.7 Demographic Characteristics of Respondents by Level of Qualification

	R.E.Degree/ Diploma (N=174)	Theology (N=101)	Teacher Training (N=89)	R.E.Post-grad Dip (N=104)	Other/ None (N=211)	Total (N=679)
Gender:						
Male	13.1%	31.8%	11.3%	12.0%	31.8%	100%
Female	34.2%	3.3%	14.6%	17.6%	30.4%	100%
Age:						
Less than 31 years	51.3%	13.1%	12.0%	6.3%	17.0%	100%
31-40 years	20.7%	18.6%	19.1%	16.0%	25.6%	100%
41-50 years	19.1%	15.8%	10.4%	19.1%	35.6%	100%
51+years	11.6%	11.6%	8.5%	20.9%	47.3%	100%
Status:						
Lay person	30.0%	7.9%	18.5%	13.1%	30.6%	100%
Priest	9.6%	82.2%	--	--	8.2%	100%
Religious Sister	24.2%	3.9%	9.2%	24.8%	38.0%	100%
Religious Brother	18.9%	2.7%	--	16.2%	62.2%	100%
Province:						
Leinster (excl. Dublin)	33.6%	17.2%	2.5%	13.1%	33.6%	100%
Dublin	38.6%	15.8%	2.6%	23.7%	19.3%	100%
Munster	25.3%	14.0%	4.3%	23.7%	32.8%	100%
Connaught	22.5%	19.7%	4.2%	11.3%	42.2%	100%
Ulster (part of)	20.5%	23.1%	7.7%	5.1%	43.6%	100%
Northern Ireland	8.5%	7.7%	53.1%	3.8%	26.9%	100%

A number of salient points may be made from these findings. Firstly, males were more likely to cite theology as their principal qualification, compared with female respondents, who, in general, had a higher proportion of catechetical qualifications. More than half (52%) of the female respondents, for instance, had a Religious Education Degree/Diploma or Post-graduate Diploma compared with one-quarter (25%) of their male counterparts. No gender differences were noted in the "Teacher Training" or "Other/None" categories.

Secondly, the age of respondents had a direct bearing on their qualifications. More than half (51%) of the youngest age group (<31 years) had a Religious Education Degree/Diploma compared with 12% of respondents over 51 years of age. Conversely, almost half (47%) of the respondents in the oldest age group (51+ years) had no formal qualifications, compared with 17% of the youngest respondents.

Thirdly, the vast majority (82%) of priests cited Theology as their principal formal Religious Education qualification. Almost two-thirds (62%) of religious brothers had no formal qualifications, compared with 38% of religious sisters and 31% of lay teachers.

Fourthly, a higher proportion of teachers in the Dublin area had formal catechetical qualifications than in other regions. In addition, a significantly higher proportion of respondents in Northern Ireland than in the other regions cited "Teacher Training" as their formal qualification.

1.4.5   In-service Courses Completed by Respondents

Respondents were asked to list any in-service courses which they may have completed over the past five years. Fifty-three per cent of respondents stated that they had attended at least one in-service course throughout the designated period. More specific details of the type of courses attended most frequently by Religious Education teachers can be found in Table 1.8 below.

Table 1.8   In-service Courses Completed by Respondents over the Past Five Years

Courses	Number	% of Total (N=546)
Teaching Methods	105	19.2%
Social Issues	97	17.8%
Texts	93	17.0%
Catechetics	54	9.9%
Doctrinal Theology	50	9.2%
Bible	45	8.2%
Syllabus	43	7.9%
Spirituality	32	5.9%
Sex Education	22	4.0%
Christology	3	0.5%
Ecclesiology	2	0.4%
Total	546	100.0%

Neither age nor status of respondent played any role in the propensity to take in-service courses. This was not the case, however, with gender of respondents. Female teachers were, on average, three times more likely than males to have completed in-service courses on any topic.

Table 1.9 provides details of the stated duration of in-service courses.

Most (83%) in-service courses were of one month's duration or less. Approximately one-third (38%) of the courses whose duration was more than one week were completed by lay people.

Table 1.9 Duration of In-service Courses

Duration	Number	% of Total (N=546)
1 day	141	25.8%
2 days - 1 week	219	40.1%
More than 1 week - 1 month	97	17.8%
More than 1 month - 3 months	21	3.8%
More than 3 months - 6 months	12	2.2%
More than 6 months - 1 year	25	4.6%
More than 1 year	31	5.7%
Total	546	100.0%

The majority (93%) of those who had completed courses found them helpful; only 7% found them unhelpful.

1.4.6   Other Subjects Taught
When asked to specify what other subjects they presently teach, a considerable range of subjects were listed. The most frequently cited subjects are given below.

	Number
Languages	391
Social	326
Science/Mathematics/Computers	148
Business	72
Music	41
Physical Education	28
Art	21
Other	21
None	84

1.4.7 Geographical Background of Respondents
Respondents were located throughout the Republic of Ireland and Northern Ireland. The distribution of respondents by state and province are listed in Table 1.10 overleaf.

Table 1.10 Respondents' Location by Province and State

Province	Number	% of Total (N=679)
Republic of Ireland:		
Dublin	115	16.9%
Leinster (excluding Dublin)	122	18.0%
Munster	186	27.4%
Connaught	71	10.5%
Ulster (part of)	39	5.7%
Northern Ireland	130	19.1%
Unknown*	16	2.3%
Total	679	100.0%

Note: In the table above, Dublin is treated separately from Leinster; Ulster includes Cavan, Monaghan and Donegal. Northern Ireland includes the six counties of Armagh, Antrim, Derry, Down, Fermanagh and Tyrone.

When comparing provinces in subsequent tables, the following categories will be used:

	Number	% of Total (N=676)
Republic of Ireland	546[10]	80.7%
Northern Ireland	130	19.2%

Details of the geographical environment in which respondents were based are outlined in the following table.

Table 1.11 Location of Schools

Location	Number	% of Total (N=665*)
Rural	116	17.4%
Small Town	207	31.1%
Large Town	147	22.1%
Suburban Area	82	12.3%
City	113	17.0%
Total	665	100.0%

* Fourteen respondents did not indicate the location of their school

Respondents were asked to indicate the type of school in which they taught Religious Education. The majority of respondents taught in secondary schools either in the Republic of Ireland or in Northern Ireland. The remaining four types of schools accounted for only one-third of the sample. The proportions of respondents in each school type are to be found in Table 1.12 below.

Table 1.12 Type of School

Type of School	Number	% of Total (N=668*)
Republic of Ireland:		
Secondary School	368	55.1%
Community / Comprehensive	77	11.5%
V.E.C. Community College	32	4.8%
V.E.C. Vocational College	66	9.9%
Northern Ireland:		
Grammar School	47	7.0%
Secondary School - N. I.	78	11.7%
Total	668	100.0%

* Eleven respondents did not indicate their school type

1.4.8 Comparison with National Profile of Religious Education Teachers

The characteristics of respondents in this sample in terms of gender, status, Religious Education qualifications, type of school and school province were found to be typical in many respects to those of Religious Education teachers in the national profile (outlined in detail in Appendix I). Some differences between the two groups were, however, apparent. This was particularly true in relation to the status and formal qualifications of respondents. For example, lay teachers were found to be under-represented in the sample where they comprised 61% of all respondents, compared with 71% in the national profile. Conversely, religious sisters were over-represented in the sample (23%), compared with their counterparts in the national profile (16%). In addition, teachers with formal Religious Education qualifications were over-represented in the sample, when compared with their colleagues as a whole throughout the country. This latter difference may be partly explained by the close relationship which exists between the number of hours taught and the possession of formal Religious Education qualifications (c.f. Table 1.6). A small number of teachers returned questionnaires unanswered as they felt that teaching Religious Education for one or two hours a week did not qualify them as Religious Education teachers.

The proportions of secondary schools in both samples were approximately equal. However, there was a higher proportion of community /comprehensive schools in the sample (11.5%), compared with 1% in the national profile. There was also a higher proportion of grammar schools in the national sample (7%) than was the case in the national profile (3%). On the other hand, vocational colleges appeared much less frequently (10%) in the sample than in the national profile (27%).

Northern Ireland was over-represented in the sample with 19% of respondents stating the location of their school to be in Northern Ireland, by comparison with 13% in the national profile.

A breakdown of demographic characteristics of respondents in this sample contrasted with those of Religious Education teachers in the national sample is presented in Table 1.13 opposite.

Table 1.13   Demographic Breakdown of Religious Education Teachers
in National Sample and National Profile

Variables	National Sample (N=679)	National Profile (N=4,565)
Gender:		
Female	59.3%	58.3%
Male	40.7%	41.7%
Status:		
Lay	60.6%	70.9%
Priest	10.9%	9.2%
Religious Brother	5.5%	4.3%
Religious Sister	23.0%	15.6%
Catechetical Qualifications:[11]		
Yes	54.0%	44.4%
No/No Response	46.0%	55.6%
Type of School:		
Republic of Ireland:		
Secondary School	55.1%	52.5%
Community / Comprehensive	11.5%	1.4%
V.E.C. Community College	4.8%	6.4%
V.E.C. Vocational College	9.9%	26.7%
Northern Ireland:		
Grammar School	7.0%	3.1%
Secondary School	11.7%	9.9%
State/Province:		
Dublin	16.9%	21.7%
Leinster (excluding Dublin)	18.0%	21.7%
Munster	27.4%	28.7%
Connaught	10.5%	10.9%
Ulster (part of)	5.7%	4.0%
Northern Ireland	19.1%	12.9%

1.4.8   Concluding Comment

The general picture of the respondents' personal characteristics which
emerged from this section indicates that respondents were quite evenly
distributed throughout the age spectrum; over half (59%) were female;
and almost two-thirds (61%) were lay persons – the remainder were

religious personnel. Respondents were shown to have varying amounts of teaching experience; more than half (54%) held a catechetical qualification for teaching Religious Education; the vast majority (86%) had spent more than one year completing their training; over half (51%) had completed their Religious Education training since 1980. Fifty-three per cent of respondents had attended at least one in-service course over the past five years; most (85%) courses were of one month's duration or less; the majority (93%) found them helpful. The majority (81%) of respondents taught in schools in the Republic of Ireland; most (67%) taught in secondary schools.

The variations between the group of teachers who responded to the questionnaire and the national profile of teachers outlined in Appendix I should be kept in mind when reading the Report. However, in order to present an objective and accurate picture, any significant differences which emerge between the respondents in terms of status, gender, formal qualifications, location and so forth will be highlighted in the text.

Notes:

1. The scope of the survey included all schools in the Republic of Ireland and Northern Ireland which were under Catholic management and/or contained a majority of Catholic pupils in 1989. (Appendix I).

2. See, for instance, the following publications: Fogarty, Ryan, Lee (Eds.) *The Irish Report of the European Value Systems Study*, Dominican Publications, 1984; Breslin, A. & Weafer, J. *Religious Beliefs, Practice, and Moral Attitudes: A Comparison of Two Irish Surveys, 1974-1984*, Council for Research and Development, Maynooth, 1984; MacMahon, B. *A Study of Dimensions of Religion Among Roman Catholic Adolescents Living in Dublin*, Ph.D. Dissertation, University of Manchester, 1981; Inglis, T. *A Study of Religious Practice, Attitudes and Beliefs of Irish University Students 1976*, Council for Research and Development, Maynooth, 1978.

3. It is not clear whether these critical attitudes are entirely attributable to a general disillusionment with Church structures or to a combination of this trend and the increasing openness of young people to speak out frankly on issues which affect their lives. For a review of the attitudes of some young people to their Church, see *Young People and the Church* (1989) by the Irish Inter-Church Meeting.

4. In the case of the Republic of Ireland, this list excluded twenty-two Protestant secondary schools, one Jewish school and five State schools under Protestant management.

5. For comparative purposes, a profile of 4,565 Religious Education teachers working in 773 Catholic post-primary schools in the Republic of Ireland and Northern Ireland was obtained and an account of the Profile is presented in Appendix I of this Report. The 773 schools which comprise the National Profile represents 85% of the total number of all Catholic post-primary schools in Ireland.

6. Sixty per cent of male respondents were lay teachers, 27% were priests and 14% were religious brothers. In relation to female respondents, 61% were found to be lay teachers while 39% were religious sisters.

7. Many respondents listed more than one qualification. For the sake of clarity of presentation and subsequent analysis, each respondent was graded according to his/her highest catechetical qualification. A large proportion of respondents with a Religious Education qualification had, for instance, also completed an extra-mural course. However, only persons whose highest form of qualification was an extra-mural course are classified under this heading in Table 1.5.

8. Respondents who were categorised as having a formal qualification in Religious Education comprised three distinct groups: 174 respondents who had completed either the B.A. Theol. in Maynooth, the three year diploma or four year degree in Mater Dei, or the one year full-time course in Mount Oliver; 101 respondents with degrees in theology; 89 respondents who had received Religious Education qualifications in the course of their teacher training studies in St. Mary's and St. Joseph's Training Colleges (Northern Ireland).

9. Respondents who had completed a part-time diploma in Religious Education (U.C.D., U.C.C.) were classified as having semi-formal qualifications.

10. Respondents in the Republic of Ireland include 13 who did not indicate the specific location of their school.

11. People were judged to have formal qualifications if they had a specific catechetical qualification, theology or a certificate received during teacher training.

Respondents' Experience of Teaching Religious Education

2.1 Introduction

Chapter Two investigates the experiences, perceptions, motivations and commitment of Religious Education teachers. The chapter also examines changes which may have occurred in respondents' perceptions of their role as Religious Education teachers. On a more practical level, the chapter goes on to look at the experiences of respondents in specific classes and the difficulties encountered by respondents in the presentation of particular topics.

2.2 Experience of Teaching Religious Education

Respondents were asked to select in order of priority from a list of given descriptions the three statements which came closest to their experiences of teaching Religious Education. A list of these descriptions, as well as the percentage of responses are outlined in Table 2.1 below. On the whole, respondents were found to be quite positive about their experiences as Religious Education teachers. The majority of teachers felt the experience of teaching Religious Education was a rewarding experience, even if for most of them it was also quite challenging. However, a substantial minority of teachers (38%) perceived the experience of teaching Religious Education as difficult and almost one in ten of the total group usually found it a very difficult experience (Table 2.1).

Table 2.1   Experience of Teaching Religious Education

	First Preference	Second Preference	Third Preference
It's a rewarding experience	7.2% (N=49)	29.0% (N=172)	23.0% (N=118)
It's a challenging but rewarding experience	51.8% (N=351)	25.4% (N=151)	7.8% (N=40)
Alright, but difficult at times	29.0% (N=196)	23.6% (N=140)	34.2% (N=176)
I just manage to get through it	2.1% (N=14)	12.0% (N=71)	14.0% (N=72)
I find it very difficult	4.6% (N=31)	4.5% (N=27)	9.7% (N=50)
I wish I could give it up	2.4% (N=16)	2.9% (N=17)	4.7% (N=24)
Other	2.9% (N=20)	2.6% (N=16)	6.6% (N=34)

Responses to this question tended to vary according to respondents' Religious Education qualifications: 63% of respondents with formal qualifications said they generally found the experience rewarding, compared with 61% of respondents with semi-formal qualifications and 38% of respondents with no qualifications. Conversely, only a small minority of qualified respondents usually found the experience difficult: 6% of respondents with formal qualifications found teaching Religious Education a generally difficult experience, compared with 11% of respondents with semi-formal qualifications and 18% of respondents with no formal qualifications. The respondents who stated in their first preference choice that they found the experience of teaching Religious Education difficult (9%) were more likely than the total group to find teaching this subject less satisfying than teaching other subjects. In addition, they were more likely to have considered giving up teaching Religious Education, to feel obliged to teach Religious Education, to feel inadequately prepared to teach this subject and to have experienced a negative change in teaching.

No significant differences emerged in respondents' replies to this question when analysed by age, gender, religious-lay status, or geographical location.

On being asked to elaborate on their experience of teaching Religious Education, the largest group of respondents (N=155) stated that "pupils were not interested". This was summed up by one respondent who stated:

"The challenge lies in the area of stimulation. Most senior students are apparently bored and the difficulty lies in arousing interest." (45 year old male lay teacher, no formal qualifications).

A further one hundred and twenty-six respondents stated that it was a "challenge to reach youth". One respondent described the situation as follows:

"It is challenging because students question facts and faith. Life is changing and always presenting new experiences that must be looked at." (30 year old female lay teacher, professionally qualified).

The following are a list of the most frequently cited statements made by respondents when asked to elaborate on their experience of teaching Religious Education:

"Pupils are not interested" (mentioned by 155 respondents)
"It is a challenge to reach youth" (126)
"Preparation is difficult" (85)
"It depends on the class" (68)

"It is rewarding when results are achieved" (56)
"Some topics are difficult to teach" (51)
"I enjoy teaching Religious Education" (51)
"There are not enough resources for Religious Education" (43)
"It is difficult to motivate students with no exam" (40)
"It is rewarding to hand on the faith" (39)
"Religious Education is important for students" (37)
"It is good when pupils question their lifestyles" (36)
"It is difficult when you are not trained" (35)
"You have to meet the needs of the class" (35)
"Pupils are anti-religion" (31)
"It makes you challenge your own values" (31)
"Aspects of teaching are rewarding" (30)
"It is very demanding work" (25)
"Pupils view Religious Education as a doss class" (21)
"The background of students is very important" (19)

The vast majority (77%) of respondents felt that their experience of teaching Religious Education varied from class to class (Table 2.2).

Table 2.2   Experience of Teaching Religious Education Varies from Class to Class

	Number	% of Total (N=625)
Yes	484	77.4%
No	141	22.6%
Total	625	100.0%

When the responses to this question were analysed by respondents' gender, school type, geographical location and age, no significant differences were found. A difference did, however, emerge when responses were analysed by respondents' qualifications. In classes of qualified personnel, 81% of respondents with formal Religious Education qualifications and 80% of respondents with semi-formal qualifications said their experience varied from class to class, compared with 56% of respondents with no formal Religious Education qualifications.

Respondents listed a wide variety of factors upon which this variance from class to class depended. The following were those which were most frequently mentioned:

"Depends on the year level of pupils" (mentioned by 142 respondents[1])
"Depends on the ability of students" (120)
"Depends on the motivation/interest of pupils" (80)
"Depends on the spirit of the class" (62)
"Depends on the discipline of the class" (42)
"No two classes are ever the same" (39)

It is evident from the above that the largest number (N=142) of respondents felt that their experience depended on the year level of pupils. One teacher commented as follows:

"I find it extremely difficult at senior level because the pupils are so apathetic and so closed in their attitudes and opinions, so I achieve very little." (24 year old female lay teacher, professionally qualified).

A similar number (N=120) of respondents felt that their experience varied according to the ability of students, as indicated by one teacher:

"Often the weaker grades find the doctrine difficult to comprehend, while the brighter streams want logical and rational argument and cannot comprehend 'mystery' or 'faith'." (29 year old female lay teacher, professionally qualified).

Respondents were asked to state whether they found teaching Religious Education more or less satisfying than teaching other subjects. The findings presented in Table 2.3 below illustrate that approximately equal percentages of respondents found Religious Education to be more satisfying, less satisfying or about the same as other subjects.

Table 2.3 Teaching Religious Education is More or Less Satisfying than Teaching Other Subjects

	Number	% of Total (N=614)
More Satisfying	185	30.1%
About the Same	214	34.9%
Less Satisfying	198	32.2%
Don't Know	17	2.8%
Total	614	100.0%

The respondents who found the experience of teaching Religious Education less satisfying than teaching other subjects comprised a higher proportion of males (37%) than females (30%); more teachers who were teaching for "three years or less" (42%) than for those teaching "four to seven years" (30%), "eight to ten years" (28%), "eleven to fifteen years" (27%), "sixteen to twenty years" (34%) and "twenty one years and over" (31%); a higher proportion of religious brothers (42%) and lay teachers (35%) than religious sisters (25%) and priests (15%); more respondents with no formal Religious Education qualifications (57%) than with semi-formal (32%) or formal (25%) qualifications. Finally, a higher proportion of respondents who found the subject less satisfying than other subjects (60%) had considered giving up teaching Religious Education than their counterparts who found teaching Religious Education more satisfying (26%) or about the same (23%).

2.3   Motivation of Respondent for Teaching Religious Education

In order to assess the motivation and commitment of Religious Education teachers to their work, respondents were asked to select, in order of priority, from a list of given descriptions, the three statements which came closest to explaining why they continued to teach Religious Education. Their responses, outlined in Table 2.4, indicate that the majority of respondents continue to teach Religious Education because they have a personal interest in the subject. However, it is interesting to note that more than one in ten respondents cited their principals' orders as their major reason for continuing to teach Religious Education.

Table 2.4 Reasons for Continuing to Teach Religious Education

	First Priority Choice	Second Priority Choice	Third Priority Choice
It's a career, like any other	3.0% (N=20)	6.6% (N=34)	29.1% (N=109)
Personal interest in teaching generally	19.6% (N=132)	50.7% (N=262)	15.2% (N=57)
Personal interest in teaching R.E.	52.4% (N=352)	25.5% (N=132)	11.8% (N=44)
I am not trained for anything else	1.0% (N=7)	2.9% (N=15)	8.8% (N=33)
I am obliged to teach R.E. by my principal	10.9% (N=73)	6.0% (N=31)	14.7% (N=55)
Other	13.1% (N=81)	8.3% (N=47)	20.4% (N=76)

The perceived importance of teaching Religious Education for the majority of respondents was also evident in the proportion of respondents (63%) who had never seriously considered giving up teaching Religious Education (Table 2.5)[2].

Table 2.5   Respondents Have Seriously Considered Giving Up Teaching Religious Education

	Number	% of Total (N=650)
Yes	241	37.1%
No	409	62.9%
Total	650	100.0%

The respondents who had seriously considered giving up teaching Religious Education comprised a higher proportion of persons aged 30 years or less (44%) than those aged 31-40 years (39%), 41-50 years (35%), or those over 50 years (30%); more respondents without formal Religious Education qualifications (47%) than respondents with formal (37%) or semi-formal (34%) qualifications; a higher proportion of lay respondents (43%) than priests (34%), religious sisters (29%) or religious brothers (11%). Geographical location, school type or respondents' gender had no significant effect on the answers given.

In addition to these demographic trends, respondents who had seriously considered giving up teaching Religious Education were also more likely than the total group of respondents to find teaching Religious Education less satisfying than teaching other subjects, to have experienced a change of motivation over the years, to have encountered topics in Religious Education which they found difficult to teach, to believe they were not professionally prepared to teach Religious Education and to feel that any changes which have occurred since they began teaching were generally for worse rather than better. In addition, these respondents are less likely than the total group of respondents to think that Religious Education had a high profile in the school among administration, staff and pupils.

Respondents were asked to explain why they would/would not consider giving up teaching Religious Education. Among the explanations offered by those respondents who did not want to give up teaching Religious Education were the following:

"I enjoy teaching Religious Education" (mentioned by 121 respondents)
"It is an important responsibility" (56)
"It is my vocation" (52)
"I have no choice" (30)
"I see it as a means of evangelisation" (29)
"I feel it is my duty" (16)
"It is what I am qualified for" (14)

Two respondents, in stating their reasons for continuing to teach Religious Education, made the following comments:

"I am glad to have the privilege of teaching Religious Education and would be sorry if I were not given a class to teach. I feel that my enthusiasm for it rubs off on many of them." (54 year old teaching sister, no formal qualifications).

"I love teaching (or trying to teach) Religion. I feel that even if the students don't respond as I would like now, I am giving them something important that will be with them for the rest of their lives." (27 year old female lay teacher, professionally qualified).

Respondents who had considered the possibility of leaving Religious Education also offered a variety of explanations:

"It is tiring/demanding" (mentioned by 46 respondents)
"I would prefer to teach less Religious Education" (35)
"I have no/very little training" (34)
"School is not a good environment" (32)
"I dislike teaching seniors" (30)
"I feel I am not doing enough" (22)

Some of the comments made by these respondents are listed below:

"I feel Religious Education is something one can only teach short term, i.e., ten years, it's personally draining and demanding." (23 year old female lay teacher, professionally qualified).

"It is one of the most difficult subjects to teach." (42 year old male lay teacher, professionally qualified).

2.4   Changes in the Role of Religious Education Teachers

All teachers in the sample were requested to stipulate whether their experience of teaching Religious Education had changed in any way since they began to teach the subject. The findings presented in Table 2.6 show that the vast majority (81%) of respondents had experienced some changes in their work.

Table 2.6   Respondents' Experience of Teaching Religious Education
Has Changed Since They Began to Teach the Subject

	Number	% of Total (N=623)
Yes	503	80.7%
No	120	19.3%
Total	623	100.0%

Over half (59%) of the respondents believed that this change in experience had been a positive one; only 16% felt it had been a negative change.

Table 2.7   Respondents' Experience of Teaching Religious Education
has Changed For Better or For Worse

	Number	% of Total (N=504)
For Better	296	58.7%
For Worse	79	15.7%
Mixed	129	25.6%
Total	504	100.0%

Not surprisingly, Religious Education teachers in the lowest age group (under 31 years) were less likely than all other age categories to state that their experience of teaching Religious Education had changed since they began teaching the subject. Other differences noted included the above average tendency for unqualified respondents to believe the change had been for worse rather than better, the significantly lower proportion of priests than other categories who considered the change was for worse, and the higher proportion of respondents who had been teaching more than sixteen years who perceived the change in a negative way.

Respondents were asked to explain the changes which they had experienced in teaching Religious Education. The response that was mentioned most frequently (30%) was that Religious Education teachers were more in tune with youth, as indicated by the following comment:

"I have learned a lot about teenagers and how to break down articles of our faith into their simple language." (29 year old priest, qualifications in theology).

However, the belief that pupils were less interested now than in previous years was also mentioned quite frequently (14%).

"Far less interest is shown nowadays. Students complain that practically every topic is boring." (54 year old male lay teacher, no formal qualifications).

"I find a marked change in the senior classes from 1980 until today: less interest. I doubt my ability to teach Religious Education effectively." (58 year old teaching sister, professionally qualified).

Table 2.8 below details the types of changes which were mentioned most frequently.

Table 2.8 Perceived Changes in Experience of Teaching Religious Education

	Number	% of Responses	% of Respondents*
More in tune with youth	191	30.4%	39.4%
Pupils are less interested	89	14.2%	18.4%
Teacher more confident	53	8.4%	10.9%
Teacher's approach has changed	49	7.8%	10.1%
Resources are better	44	7.0%	9.1%
Teacher less interested	42	6.7%	8.7%
Teacher more interested	31	4.9%	6.4%
Pupils more interested	28	4.5%	5.8%
Society has changed	26	4.1%	5.4%
Course is more relevant	21	3.3%	4.3%

* Note: In this and similar tables, respondents were given the opportunity to make more than one response. Consequently, the total percentage in this column is greater than 100% as respondents may have made up to three responses.

In a similar vein, more than half (52%) of the respondents felt that their motivation for teaching Religious Education had changed over the years (Table 2.9).

Table 2.9   Respondents' Motivation for Teaching Religious Education
Has Changed Over the Past Years

	Number	% of Total (N=633)
Yes	332	52.4%
No	301	47.6%
Total	633	100.0%

It is clear from the responses outlined below that in many cases (N=237), the change in motivation experienced by respondents has in fact been a positive one.

"Religious Education is more important to me now" (mentioned by 86 respondents)
"Pupils are less interested now" (59)
"Realise the importance of Religious Education for youth" (53)
"I am not as motivated as I was" (46)
"Content of the course has changed" (38)
"My style of teaching has changed" (35)
"Resources are better now" (25)
"I am more experienced now" (21)
"I am more realistic now" (18)
"I have a greater desire to share faith" (18)
"I am more confident now" (16)

Some random comments were as follows:

"The lack of interest among pupils in general has dampened my enthusiasm. I go to the trouble of preparing lessons and then find that I'm not satisfied with the reaction of the class." (55 year old teaching sister, professionally qualified).

"It is difficult to deal with apathy and a reluctance to participate among students. Doing some work, putting some thought into the classes is out for many students." (33 year old female lay teacher, no formal qualifications).

"Now, I am more committed. I see that the newer approach in primary school has made people more conscious of their Christianity. I suppose I also personally find a joy/peace in knowing God that I wish all could share." (43 year old male lay teacher, professionally qualified).

"I am more motivated now than previously. I learned how to relate to the pupils on a deeper level and with trust. It makes the job more interesting." (34 year old female lay teacher, professionally qualified).

"Yes, it has got stronger. From a shaky start, I have grown in confidence; over the past few years I have found that I go into class without tension or fear in myself. I know what I'm at and my own programme seems to work especially for seniors." (39 year old priest, qualifications in theology).

2.5 Practical Experiences of Teaching Religious Education

Respondents were asked to recall one particular worthwhile religion class which they had taught and to describe the subject matter of the class, the ability of pupils in the class as well as the year to which the class was taught. Tables 2.10, 2.11 and 2.12 detail responses to these questions.

Table 2.10   Subject of Worthwhile Religion Class

	Number	% of Total (N=585)
Social Problems	100	17.1%
Doctrinal Theology	96	16.4%
Sexuality	69	11.8%
Sacraments	67	11.5%
Spirituality	54	9.2%
Christology	43	7.3%
Bible	37	6.3%
Personal Development	35	6.0%
Ecclesiology	22	3.8%
Vocations	21	3.6%
Other Religions	10	1.7%
Texts	3	0.5%
Other	28	4.8%
Total	585	100.0%

It is clear from Table 2.10 that the subject matter of worthwhile classes varied considerably between respondents. In relation to the ability of pupils in the classes mentioned as worthwhile, it was found that classes with pupils of low ability were mentioned as worthwhile less frequently (12%) than those with pupils of mixed (40%), medium (26%) or high ability (23%). With the exception of 4th Year, all other years were represented in approximately equal percentages.

Table 2.11   Ability of Pupils in Worthwhile Religion Class

	Number	% of Total (N=585)
High	132	22.6%
Medium	150	25.6%
Low	71	12.1%
Mixed	232	39.7%
Total	585	100.0%

Table 2.12   Year Group of Worthwhile Religion Class

	Number	% of Total (N=585)
1st Year	94	16.0%
2nd Year	99	16.9%
3rd Year	123	21.0%
4th Year	38	6.5%
5th Year	123	21.0%
6th Year	104	17.7%
Transition Year	4	0.8%
Total	585	100.0%

Respondents were found to use a variety of methods in teaching Religious Education (Table 2.13). Books and experiential methods were used most frequently in teaching the class respondents mentioned as worthwhile.

Table 2.13   Method of Teaching Used

	Number	% of Responses	% of Respondents
Book	238	28.4%	45.9%
Experiential	219	26.1%	42.2%
Visual	164	19.6%	31.6%
Audio	156	18.6%	30.1%
Other	61	7.3%	11.8%

Respondents were given the opportunity to describe any 'other' methods which they used in teaching Religious Education. The following are those which were mentioned most frequently:

"Discussion Groups" (mentioned by 142 respondents)
"Books not on syllabus" (49)
"Role play" (30)
"Personal Experiences" (28)
"Video" (21)
"Handouts" (17)
"Questions and Answers" (14)
"Songs" (10)

In response to the question "Why do you think the class was worthwhile for the pupils?", the most frequently cited response (57%) was that it was interesting and relevant, as indicated by the following comments of two teachers:

"They [pupils] were fully involved in the lesson and were responsive and enthusiastic about the topic." (40 year old teaching sister, qualifications in theology).

"They [pupils] participated almost 100% and expressed satisfaction." (53 year old teaching sister, no formal qualifications).

Other responses mentioned were that the class was worthwhile for pupils because it was a learning experience (17%), or because it contributed to the spiritual development of the pupils (10%).

"It helped to make Jesus real for them and made a relationship with him possible." (62 year old priest, qualifications in theology).

Table 2.14 outlines these responses in further detail.

Table 2.14   Reason Why Class was Perceived as Worthwhile for Pupils

	Number	% of Responses	% of Respondents
Interesting and relevant	498	56.6%	85.4%
Learning experience	150	17.0%	25.7%
Spiritual development	85	9.7%	14.6%
Personal development	84	9.5%	14.4%
Way it was taught	40	4.5%	6.9%
Social learning experience	20	2.3%	3.4%
Other	3	0.3%	0.5%

Respondents were also asked to describe why they felt that the class was worthwhile for themselves. The results presented in Table 2.15 seem to indicate that most Religious Education teachers consider a class to be worthwhile when it is of benefit to pupils rather than to themselves. For example, the belief that the class was worthwhile because pupils found it to be interesting was mentioned far more frequently (32%) than that it was worthwhile because they (i.e., teachers) were interested (3%). Likewise, the fact that it was worthwhile because it was a learning experience for pupils was mentioned more frequently (7%) than that it had been a learning experience for themselves (3%).

Table 2.15 Reason Why Class was Worthwhile for Teacher

	Number	% of Responses	%of Respondents
Pupils were interested	287	32.4%	50.0%
It worked/class was a success	141	15.9%	24.6%
Spiritual Development of pupils	74	8.4%	12.9%
Openness of the class	71	8.0%	12.4%
Learning experience for pupils	64	7.2%	11.1%
Teacher learned about youth	51	5.8%	8.9%
Personal development of pupils	43	4.9%	7.5%
Spiritual development of teacher	33	3.7%	5.7%
Teacher was interested	30	3.4%	5.2%
Way it was taught	27	3.1%	4.7%
Giving necessary information	24	2.7%	4.2%
Learning experience for teacher	24	2.7%	4.2%
Other	16	1.2%	1.9%

2.6 Difficulties Encountered by Religious Education Teachers
In order to assess problems which Religious Education Teachers encounter in their work, respondents were asked whether there were any topics in Religious Education which they found difficult to teach. As Table 2.16 demonstrates, over half (53%) of the respondents found difficulty with some subjects.

Table 2.16   Respondents Find Topics in Religious Education Difficult
to Teach

	Number	% of Total (N=608)
Yes	324	53.3%
No	284	46.7%
Total	608	100.0%

Respondents' ages and level of formal qualifications were found to
have a significant impact on the answers to this question. A higher proportion of younger respondents and those with formal qualifications
found difficulty with some topics than did other respondents who were
older and without Religious Education qualifications.

Respondents were asked to list the topics which presented difficulty to
them. Sexuality was the area which presented most difficulty to Religious Education teachers. Teaching the sacraments also presented problems for teachers; the same was true for the area of doctrinal theology.
Table 2.17 details these findings in greater detail.

Table 2.17   Topics which Present Difficulty to Religious Education
Teachers

	Number	% of Responses	% of Respondents
Sexuality	191	20.8%	57.0%
Sacraments	173	18.8%	51.6%
Doctrinal Theology	142	15.5%	42.4%
Social Issues	99	10.8%	29.6%
Bible	91	9.9%	27.2%
Ecclesiology	71	7.7%	21.2%
Spiritual Issues	66	7.2%	19.7%
Other Religions/Cults	22	2.4%	6.6%
Personal Development	17	1.9%	5.1%
Christology	15	1.6%	4.5%
Texts	3	0.3%	0.9%
Other	28	3.1%	8.4%

Tables 2.18 and 2.19 opposite outline the stream and year level of pupils
with which Religious Education teachers found difficulty in teaching

certain topics. While it is clear from Table 2.18 that stream level of pupils had little effect on the level of difficulty experienced in teaching certain topics, this was not the case with year level. Senior level was mentioned far more frequently (mentioned by 444 respondents) than other year levels in relation to topics which posed difficulty for Religious Education teachers (Table 2.19).

Table 2.18   Stream Level to which Difficult Subjects were Taught

	Number	% of Responses	% of Respondents
Upper and Lower	407	69.6%	128.0%
Lower	106	18.1%	33.3%
Upper	72	12.3%	22.6%

Table 2.19   Year level to which Difficult Subjects were Taught

	Number	% of Responses	% of Respondents
Senior	444	54.1%	140.5%
Junior	197	24.0%	62.3%
Junior and Senior	179	21.8%	56.7%

Respondents offered a number of explanations for the difficulties which they experienced. The largest number of teachers (N=156) attributed their difficulty to a lack of interest on the part of pupils. The following comments were typical of those who expressed this opinion.

"The students aren't switched on by scripture and it's a constant battle to hold their attention." (34 year old priest, qualifications in theology).

"At senior level, any topic that seems to be in any way linked with 'God' or 'formal religious instruction' turns pupils off completely, and thus makes it impossible to teach them." (24 year old female lay teacher, professionally qualified).

A similar number (N=122) of respondents said they found difficulty in explaining certain topics. One teacher stated his reason as follows:

"I feel that these topics, especially Trinity, papal infallibility and suffering are more adult topics than teenage ones." (41 year old male lay teacher, professionally qualified).

Listed below are those explanations which were offered most frequently by respondents:

"Pupils not interested" (mentioned by 156 respondents)
"Topic is difficult to explain" (122)
"Irrelevant to pupils" (106)
"Teachings not accepted by pupils" (71)
"Resources not good" (60)
"Personal dislike of topic" (50)
"Lack of knowledge of teacher" (46)
"Teacher's disagreement with Church" (40)
"Too close to pupils personal lives" (29)
"Difficult to justify Church's position" (17)

Notes:

1. Within this group, over half of the respondents (N=77) felt juniors were easier to teach than seniors.

2. Based on the results of recent surveys, the relatively high proportion (37%) of respondents who had considered giving up teaching Religious Education is indicative of the state of the teaching profession as a whole, rather than a sign of a general malaise within Religious Education teachers. An I.N.T.O. study conducted in Northern Ireland late in 1990, for instance, found that more than 88 per cent of teachers in Northern Ireland would retire from teaching if given the opportunity. Of more relevance to the present study is the survey on stress among teachers which was commissioned by the A.S.T.I., T.U.I., and I.N.T.O. and carried out during October 1990 to January 1991. A summary of this report indicates that teachers as a whole are experiencing considerable stress and that this stress is affecting their psychological well-being and intentions to leave teaching.

CHAPTER THREE

Religious Education Texts

3.1 Introduction

This chapter seeks to establish an overall picture of the perceived usefulness and general effectiveness of Religious Education texts for the teaching of Religion in Irish schools. While particular attention is focused on texts which are recommended for use in the teaching of Religious Education at post-primary level, this chapter also deals with other texts and resources used by Religious Education teachers in the course of their work.

3.2 Use of Religious Education Texts

In the first question respondents were asked to indicate whether they used Religious Education texts regularly. As may be seen in Table 3.1 below, the majority (87%) of teachers use texts regularly.

Table 3.1 Respondents Use Religious Education Texts Regularly

	Number	% of Total (N=663)
Yes	577	87.0%
No	86	13.0%
Total	663	100.0%

The 86 teachers who do not use texts regularly comprised a mixed group of respondents who were not distinguishable by age, school type, gender or geographical location. However, status of respondent and level of qualifications attained did have some effect on the use of text. Religious brothers and priests were least likely to use texts when compared with religious sisters and lay teachers. In addition, the absence of a general Religious Education qualification had a negative effect on the use of texts.

Respondents who use texts were asked to indicate the major text or series used most frequently by them in their classes. An overview of the texts used most regularly by teachers in each class level and their frequency of use is presented in Table 3.2 overleaf.

The findings presented in this table highlight the dominance of the *Christian Way Series* in the Junior Cycle and, to a lesser extent, the *Living*

Faith Series in the Senior Cycle. While particular attention is focused on the perceived merits and failings of the *Christian Way Series* in Section 3.5 following, the remainder of this section will concentrate on respondents' views of Religious Education texts in general.

Table 3.2   Religious Education Texts Used Most Frequently by Class Level

Class Level	Number of Times Mentioned	% of Class Total
First Year Texts		
Christian Way 1	347	74.5%
Walk in My Presence	33	7.1%
I Will be With You	19	4.1%
Other texts	67	14.4%
Total:	**466**	**100.0%**
Second Year Texts		
Christian Way 2	332	74.1%
Christian Way 1	57	12.7%
Pilgrims	7	1.6%
Other texts	52	11.6%
Total:	**448**	**100.0%**
Third Year Texts		
Christian Way 3	293	67.8%
Christian Way 2	67	15.5%
Pilgrims	19	4.4%
Other texts	53	12.3%
Total:	**432**	**100.0%**
Fourth Year Texts		
Living Faith Series	77	30.6%
Christian Way 3	45	17.9%
I Will Be With You Always	12	4.8%
Pilgrims	10	4.0%
Other texts	108	42.8%
Total:	**252**	**100.0%**

Table 3.2 *Continued Opposite*

Table 3.2 *Continued*

Class Level	Number of Times Mentioned	% of Class Total
Fifth Year Texts		
Living Faith Series	176	43.3%
Moral Questions	36	8.5%
You Gather a People	25	5.9%
God and Man Series	15	3.5%
I Will Be With You Always	15	3.5%
Mystery of God	12	2.8%
Sacraments and You	11	2.6%
Other texts	126	29.8%
Total:	**416**	**100.0%**
Sixth Year Texts		
Living Faith Series	56	21.0%
Moral Questions	33	12.4%
God and Man Series	20	7.5%
Mystery of God	16	6.0%
You Gather a People	13	4.9%
Finley and Pennock	11	4.1%
I Will Be With You Always	10	3.7%
Other texts	108	40.4%
Total:	**267**	**100.0%**

3.3 Perceived Usefulness of Texts

Respondents were asked to indicate how useful they found Religious Education texts in teaching Religious Education. The findings in Table 3.3 overleaf indicate that most respondents were generally satisfied with the usefulness of Religious Education texts in teaching. However, substantial proportions of respondents indicated some level of dissatisfaction when they answered "sometimes useful".

Table 3.3   Perceived Usefulness of Texts by Respondents in Each
Class Level

	Very Useful	Useful	Sometimes Useful	Not Useful	Totally Useless
First Year Texts					
Christian Way 1	20.4% (N=67)	52.0% (N=171)	22.5% (N=74)	4.6% (N=15)	0.6% (N=2)
Walk in My Presence	52.0% (N=13)	36.0% (N=9)	8.0% (N=2)	4.0% (N=1)	-- --
I Will be With You	50.0% (N=8)	31.0% (N=5)	19.0% (N=3)	-- --	-- --
Second Year Texts					
Christian Way 2	21.6% (N=62)	39.4% (N=113)	30.7% (N=88)	7.3% (N=21)	1.0% (N=3)
Christian Way 1	27.1% (N=13)	35.4% (N=17)	29.2% (N=14)	8.3% (N=4)	-- --
Pilgrims	28.6% (N=2)	28.6% (N=2)	28.6% (N=2)	14.3% (N=1)	-- --
Third Year Texts					
Christian Way 3	22.1% (N=56)	36.8% (N=93)	33.6% (N=85)	5.5% (N=14)	2.0% (N=5)
Christian Way 2	22.0% (N=11)	34.0% (N=17)	30.0% (N=15)	8.0% (N=4)	6.0% (N=3)
Pilgrims	35.7% (N=5)	28.6% (N=4)	28.6% (N=4)	7.1% (N=1)	-- --
Fourth Year Texts					
Living Faith Series	25.6% (N=10)	41.0% (N=16)	25.6% (N=10)	5.1% (N=2)	2.6% (N=1)
Christian Way 3	17.4% (N=4)	34.8% (N=8)	43.5% (N=10)	4.3% (N=1)	-- --
I Will Be With You Always	-- --	42.9% (N=3)	57.1% (N=4)	-- --	-- --

Table 3.3 *Continued Opposite*

Table 3.3   *Continued*

	Very Useful	Useful	Sometimes Useful	Not Useful	Totally Useless
Fifth Year Texts					
Living Faith Series	15.6% (N=10)	40.6% (N=26)	37.5% (N=24)	6.3% (N=4)	-- --
Moral Questions	7.1% (N=1)	42.9% (N=6)	42.9% (N=6)	7.1% (N=1)	-- --
You Gather a People	33.3% (N=3)	11.1% (N=1)	55.6% (N=5)	-- --	-- --
Sixth Year Texts					
Living Faith Series	50.0% (N=7)	35.7% (N=5)	14.3% (N=2)	-- --	-- --
Moral Questions	18.8% (N=3)	56.3% (N=9)	25.0% (N=4)	-- --	-- --
God and Man Series	33.3% (N=2)	33.3% (N=2)	16.7% (N=1)	16.7% (N=1)	-- --

Note: The relatively low number of respondents, especially in the senior years, is partly attributable to the diversity of texts used by teachers.

3.4   Most Useful and Least Useful Characteristics of Texts

In general, the characteristics of texts which appealed most to respondents were, overall presentation, use of stories, inclusion of assignments and resource material, the use of illustrations, and real life examples. Conversely, those characteristics which were perceived as least useful by respondents included the use of difficult language and concepts, the advanced and abstract nature of the contents, the use of boring and irrelevant material, the absence of illustrations and the omission of adequate details.

In addition to examining texts as a whole, respondents were asked to indicate the characteristics of specific texts which they found to be most useful and also least useful. The most frequently cited responses are listed in Table 3.4 overleaf.

Table 3.4   Most Useful and Least Useful Characteristics of Texts

Most Useful Characteristics	Least Useful Characteristics
1. Christian Way 1	
Sacraments/Baptism (N=45)	Too advanced/Difficult/Academic (N=50)
Presentation/Illustrations (N=37)	Language too difficult (N=12)
Bible History/Holy Land (N=30)	Chapter 4: Baptism (N=10)
Assignments/Resource Material (N=27)	Chapter 1: A New Community (N=8)
Stories (N=24)	Illustrations (N=8)
Teachers' Manual (N=21)	Boring (N=8)
General Content (N=20)	Irrelevant to pupils (N=5)
Overall Approach/Framework (N=18)	
Chapter 3: Mystery of Christ's Presence (N=17)	
Chapter 8: Towards Christian Unity (N=16)	
Chapter 5: Eucharist the Sacred Banquet (N=15)	
Relevant to pupils' lives (N=12)	
2. Christian Way 2	
Overall Approach (N=21)	Too Advanced (N=19)
Assignments/Resource Material (N=17)	Language too difficult (N=20)
Stories (N=13)	Boring (N=11)
Teachers' Manual (N=12)	Irrelevant to pupils (N=7)
Presentation (N=10)	Chapter 4: Long Road to Freedom (N=9)
Relevance to pupils (N=8)	Chapter Six: Going Astray (N=8)
Chapter 6: Penance (N=5)	
Chapter 9: Portrait of Our Saviour (N=5)	

Table 3.4 *Continued Opposite*

Table 3.4   *Continued*

Most Useful Characteristics	Least Useful Characteristics

3. Christian Way 3

Most Useful Characteristics	Least Useful Characteristics
Overall Approach (N=20)	Too Advanced (N=21)
Presentation (N=10)	Irrelevant to pupils' lives (N=17)
Stories (N=10)	Language too difficult (N=10)
Topics/Content (N=10)	
Resources/Assignments (N=10)	
Chapter Four (N=6)	
Chapter Three (N=5)	
Chapter One (N=4)	

4. Walk in My Presence

Most Useful Characteristics	Least Useful Characteristics
Stories (N=6)	Too Advanced (N=4)
Presentation (N=5)	Limp/Unrealistic stories (N=2)
Resource Material (N=3)	Inadequate detail (N=2)
Teachers' Book (N=3)	Chapter Three (N=2)
Experiential Approach (N=1)	Creation Section (N=2)
Variety (N=1)	
Language is understandable (N=1)	
Parents' Exercises (N=1)	

5. Living Faith Series

Most Useful Characteristics	Least Useful Characteristics
Assignments (N=9)	Too Complicated (N=13)
General Content (N=8)	Boring/Irrelevant (N=7)
Presentation (N=6)	Inadequate Content (N=6)
Relevant to Pupils (N=6)	Too Simplistic (N=5)
Choices (N=5)	Bad presentation (N=2)

3.5   The Christian Way Series

Respondents who use any part of the *Christian Way Series* (Table 3.5 below) were asked to rate the various elements of this series for both teachers and students. Their responses are outlined in Table 3.6.

Table 3.5   Respondents Use *Christian Way Series*

	Yes	No	Total
Christian Way 1	88.4%	11.6%	100%
	(N=504)	(N=66)	(N=570)
Christian Way 2	87.1%	12.9%	100%
	(N=480)	(N=71)	(N=551)
Christian Way 3	84.5%	15.5%	100%
	(N=441)	(N=81)	(N=522)
Come Follow Me	27.9%	72.1%	100%
	(N=87)	(N=225)	(N=312)

Table 3.6   Respondents' Rating of *Christian Way Series*

	Excellent	Good	Ave.	Poor	Total
Teachers' Book:					
Christian Way 1	15.3%	44.1%	30.0%	10.6%	100%
	(N=75)	(N=216)	(N=147)	(N=52)	(N=490)
Christian Way 2	14.0%	42.5%	30.5%	12.9%	100%
	(N=64)	(N=194)	(N=139)	(N=59)	(N=456)
Christian Way 3	17.7%	44.6%	26.9%	10.8%	100%
	(N=74)	(N=186)	(N=112)	(N=45)	(N=417)
Come Follow Me	15.4%	25.3%	38.5%	20.9%	100%
	(N=14)	(N=23)	(N=35)	(N=19)	(N=91)
Students' Book:					
Christian Way 1	10.0%	39.4%	31.7%	18.9%	100%
	(N=48)	(N=190)	(N=153)	(N=91)	(N=482)
Christian Way 2	8.9%	32.7%	34.2%	24.2%	100%
	(N=41)	(N=151)	(N=158)	(N=112)	(N=462)
Christian Way 3	8.5%	39.7%	35.6%	16.2%	100%
	(N=35)	(N=164)	(N=147)	(N=67)	(N=413)
Come Follow Me	6.2%	19.8%	37.0%	37.0%	100%
	(N=5)	(N=16)	(N=30)	(N=30)	(N=81)

A number of salient points may be made from the findings presented in Table 3.6 opposite. Firstly, the majority of respondents considered the teachers' version of *Christian Way 1, 2* and *3* to be "Excellent" or "Good". Conversely, only a minority considered the students' texts to be "Excellent" or "Good".

Secondly, a relatively large proportion of respondents were dissatisfied with the texts, especially in the case of *Come Follow Me*. A significantly higher proportion of respondents were dissatisfied with this latter text than was the case with the other texts.

Thirdly, while many teachers indicated satisfaction with the *Christian Way Series*, the opinions presented in Table 3.6 clearly show a high level of dissatisfaction with the Series as it is currently presented. Accordingly, respondents were asked to specify whether they would wish to see any changes if the series (*Christian Way 1, 2, 3*) was being presented again. Their responses are outlined in Table 3.7 below.

Table 3.7   *Christian Way Series* Should Be the Same or Different

	Number	% of Total (N=567)
Same	65	11.5%
Different	502	88.5%
Total	567	100.0%

Some of the most frequently-cited changes which respondents would wish to see incorporated in the *Christian Way Series* included the need to change the language of the texts, updated material which would be more relevant to the lives of young people, and the inclusion of material which would make the texts more attractive to the students. Each of these areas are discussed below.

(a)   Language and Concepts
Some general comments mentioned by respondents were:

"The language needs to be changed and made more simple" (mentioned by 113 respondents)
"The text is too difficult for weaker students ... They are geared too much to the average to bright students" (87)
"A lot of the concepts are unclear ... too abstract" (28)

Some specific comments made by individual teachers are listed below.

"Weaker students find the vocabulary very difficult." (51 year old teaching sister, no formal qualifications).

"It's far too difficult for weaker pupils ... the language is not understood by many." (30 year old female lay teacher, professionally qualified).

"The language should be more appropriate to the average student. The doctrine should be stated more concisely, and clearly differentiated from the preamble." (28 year old male lay teacher, professionally qualified).

"Language needs to be within scope of average student. Male bias could be less obvious..." (43 year old teaching sister, professionally qualified).

(b) Presentation of Text
The most frequently mentioned suggestions which related to the texts' presentation and overall layout were:
"More assignments ... practical work accompanying work sheets" (mentioned by 74 respondents)
"The texts should have a better layout and presentation" (55)
"It needs to be more concise" (24)
"Better illustrations and stories" (21)
"It needs to be livened up" (15)
"A specific question and answer section is needed" (9)
"Themes are disjointed" (7)
"Needs detailed treatment of specific topics with audio-visual aids to go with each topic" (6)

(c) Content
A large number of respondents suggested ways in which some aspect of the texts' content were deficient and could be improved upon. These comments tended to fall into one of three categories: relevance, general content and specific content. The most frequently cited comments are given below:

Relevance:
"The text should be more relevant to their age groups and to pupils' immediate lives" (mentioned by 76 respondents)
"Update the articles ... examples ... stories" (48)
"More geared towards pupils' problems" (10)

General Content:
"It needs more doctrinal material" (11)
"More scripture" (9)
"It needs more variety" (7)
"Better treatment of Sacraments" (7)
"More prayer" (7)
"More spiritual content" (6)
"More about Our Lady" (5)
"Not a lot in it ... if one relied on the texts as they are, students would have very little to chew on" (4)
"More liturgical material" (3)
"It's too spiritual" (2)

Some specific comments made by individual teachers which reflect the priorities listed above were:

"I have been using this series for six years, so I would like to see it updated but not necessarily changed ... except for the language in text book 2." (27 year old female lay teacher, no formal qualifications).

"Stories and language used should be brought up to date. Examples more relevant to today. More pictures to help those with reading difficulties." (28 year old teaching sister, professionally qualified).

3.6   Alternatives to Texts

Respondents who do not use texts were asked to specify what they use instead of Religious Education texts. The most frequently mentioned alternatives are listed below.

Alternatives to Religious Education Texts	Number of Times Mentioned
Magazines/Newspapers	52
Visual/Audio Aids	49
Own Courses/Resources	37
Bible	29
Discussion/Pupils' Experiences	26
Questionnaires/Information Sheets/Projects	18
Music/Art	11
Miscellaneous Books/Pamphlets/Techniques	66

When asked to explain why they do not use Religious Education texts, respondents gave the following explanations.

	Number of Times Mentioned
No suitable texts available	37
Boring/Unattractive/Irrelevant/Outdated	28
Texts too difficult for weaker classes	23
Prefer freedom of alternative methods and material	22
Texts unsuitable for complete course	17
Pupils spend too much time reading during the day – they need a break	12
Some topics not included	11
Pupils have little faith	6
Expensive	6
Badly presented	4

3.7   Resource Materials Used in Teaching Religious Education

All respondents were asked if they used resource materials other than texts and the vast majority (98%, N=647) said they did, while only eleven respondents did not. The three most popular resource materials used by respondents were discussion, the Bible and prayer/meditation. Conversely, the three least popular resources availed of by respondents were field work, guest speakers and audio tapes/records. The resource materials used most frequently by respondents are listed in Table 3.8 opposite.

Table 3.8 Frequency of Use of Resource Materials

Resource Materials	Frequently	Sometimes	Rarely	Never
Video	15.8% (N=107)	55.1% (N=374)	12.5% (N=85)	16.6% (N=113)
Guest Speakers	4.9% (N=33)	29.0% (N=197)	21.8% (N=148)	44.3% (N=301)
Field Work	0.9% (N=6)	8.0% (N=54)	10.6% (N=72)	80.6% (N=547)
Discussion	59.4% (N=403)	24.6% (N=167)	2.5% (N=17)	13.5% (N=92)
Prayer/Meditation	24.4% (N=166)	37.5% (N=255)	12.8% (N=87)	25.2% (N=171)
Audio tapes/records	4.3% (N=29)	31.5% (N=214)	17.5% (N=119)	46.6% (N=317)
Magazines	1.8% (N=12)	35.3% (N=240)	13.3% (N=90)	49.6% (N=337)
Bible	42.7% (N=290)	36.0% (N=245)	5.9% (N=40)	15.3% (N=104)
Experiential activities	7.2% (N=49)	22.6% (N=154)	11.2% (N=76)	58.9% (N=400)
Role Play	5.3% (N=36)	23.5% (N=160)	15.6% (N=106)	55.5% (N=377)

Respondents were also given the opportunity of specifying alternative resource materials and these are given below.

Additional Resource Materials	No of Times Mentioned
Projects/Group work	56
Art/Music/Poetry/Drama	52
Religious Devotions (Mass, Retreats, Prayer etc.)	47
Worksheets/Questionnaires/Handouts	38
Newspapers	34
Visual Aids (Slides etc.)	26
Stories/Books	18
Debating/Quiz	17
Lectures/Discussion	14

In addition to indicating the frequency with which they use resource materials, respondents were also asked to specify the extent to which they use these resources at junior and senior cycle. The largest grouping of respondents used the specified resources at both junior and senior cycles. However, some salient differences in the use of resources between junior and senior cycles included a greater emphasis on role play, audio tapes and the Bible in junior classes than in senior classes. Conversely, a higher proportion of Religious Education teachers in senior classes than in junior classes tended to use field work, magazines and video. These responses are outlined in Tables 3.9 below.

Table 3.9 Use of Resource Materials by Cycle of Classes

Resource Materials	Junior Cycle	Senior Cycle	Junior & Senior Cycle	Cycle Not Specified
Video	17.9% (N=99)	27.0% (N=149)	46.4% (N=256)	8.7% (N=48)
Guest Speakers	12.3% (N=44)	55.6% (N=199)	25.1% (N=90)	7.0% (N=25)
Field Work	25.2% (N=41)	38.7% (N=63)	29.4% (N=48)	6.7% (N=11)
Discussion	17.8% (N=100)	24.1% (N=135)	49.9% (N=280)	8.2% (N=46)
Prayer/Meditation	22.1% (N=109)	17.6% (N=87)	51.8% (N=256)	8.5% (N=42)
Audio tapes/records	26.1% (N=92)	17.0% (N=60)	48.9% (N=172)	8.0% (N=28)
Magazines	19.7% (N=83)	34.1% (N=144)	37.7% (N=159)	8.5% (N=36)
Bible	25.1% (N=142)	15.9% (N=90)	50.7% (N=287)	8.3% (N=47)
Experiential activities	20.8% (N=57)	22.3% (N=61)	50.0% (N=137)	6.9% (N=19)
Role Play	48.4% (N=152)	17.2% (N=54)	29.0% (N=91)	5.4% (N=17)

The results presented in Table 3.10 below indicate that approximately two-thirds of respondents used the specified resource materials for both upper and lower streams. However, when a distinction was made between streams, a consistently higher proportion of respondents used these resources in the upper streams than in the lower streams.

Table 3.10 Use of Resource Materials by Streaming of Classes

Resource Materials	Lower Stream	Upper Stream	Lower/ Upper	No Streaming	Stream Not Specified
Video	9.5% (N=40)	14.7% (N=62)	61.9% (N=262)	5.2% (N=22)	8.7% (N=37)
Guest Speakers	5.6% (N=16)	18.1% (N=52)	61.0% (N=175)	5.2% (N=15)	10.1% (N=29)
Field Work	8.1% (N=11)	17.8% (N=24)	61.5% (N=83)	-- --	12.6% (N=17)
Discussion	8.6% (N=36)	15.1% (N=63)	62.4% (N=260)	4.1% (N=17)	9.8% (N=41)
Prayer/Meditation	9.9% (N=37)	11.3% (N=42)	64.6% (N=241)	5.4% (N=20)	8.9% (N=32)
Audio tapes/records	8.9% (N=24)	13.0% (N=35)	64.1% (N=173)	4.1% (N=11)	10.0% (N=27)
Magazines	9.5% (N=30)	15.6% (N=49)	60.0% (N=189)	4.1% (N=13)	10.8% (N=34)
Bible	7.7% (N=32)	12.3% (N=51)	66.1% (N=273)	4.6% (N=19)	9.2% (N=38)
Experiential activities	7.7% (N=16)	13.0% (N=27)	65.4% (N=136)	3.4% (N=7)	10.6% (N=22)
Role Play	15.3% (N=36)	15.3% (N=36)	54.5% (N=128)	4.3% (N=10)	10.6% (N=25)

3.8   Topics Omitted From Course Texts

A substantial proportion (45%) of respondents felt topics were omitted from their course texts which they would like to see included as indicated in Table 3.11.

Table 3.11 Topics are Omitted From Course Text(s)

	Number	% of Total (N=432)
Yes	196	45.4%
No	234	54.2%
Don't Know	2	0.5%
Total	432	100%

Respondents listed a variety of topics which they felt should be included in course texts: the list below shows that the area which the largest number (N=76) of respondents felt should be included was that of social problems; 55 respondents felt that greater attention should be given to the area of sexuality.

"Social Problems" (mentioned by 76 respondents)
"Sexuality" (55)
"Other Religions/Cults" (38)
"Spirituality" (35)
"Doctrinal Theology" (33)
"Ecclesiology" (31)
"Personal Development" (28)
"Sacraments" (27)
"Bible" (23)
"Christology" (8)
"Youth Culture" (6)

CHAPTER FOUR

Status of Religious Education

4.1 *Introduction*

This chapter examines the status of Religious Education in the school. More particularly, it examines the profile of Religious Education among administration, staff and pupils. It details the amount of time allocated to Religious Education by the school, as well as the facilities for Religious Education teachers to discuss their subject with both colleagues and parents of pupils. It also investigates the amount of assistance which Religious Education teachers receive from principals, chaplains and diocesan advisors.

4.2 *Profile of Religious Education*

Respondents were asked whether they felt Religious Education had a high profile in the school among administration, staff, senior pupils and junior pupils. Table 4.1 demonstrates that the majority (69%) of respondents felt that Religious Education had indeed a high profile among the school administration. In contrast however, less than half (42%) believed this was the case for staff members, only 30% felt Religious Education had a high profile among senior pupils and 51.5% considered Religious Education to have a high profile among junior pupils.

Table 4.1   Religious Education has a High Profile Among Administration, Staff, and Pupils

	Yes	No	Don't Know	Total
Administration	69.2% (N=454)	20.4% (N=134)	10.4% (N=68)	100% (N=656)
Staff	41.8% (N=274)	37.7% (N=247)	20.5% (N=134)	100% (N=655)
Pupils - Senior	30.4% (N=194)	47.3% (N=302)	22.3% (N=142)	100% (N=638)
Pupils - Junior	51.5% (N=334)	30.2% (N=196)	18.3% (N=119)	100% (N=649)

An analysis of how the various sub-groups of Religious Education teachers perceived the situation is presented below.

Table 4.2   Religious Education has a High Profile Among
Administration, Staff, and Pupils by Selected Characteristics

	Administration	Staff	Senior Pupils	Junior Pupils
Age:				
Less than 30 years	58.0%	34.0%	28.0%	53.0%
31 - 40 years	71.0%	43.0%	34.0%	54.0%
41 - 50 years	73.0%	46.0%	30.0%	47.0%
More than 50 years	77.0%	43.0%	30.0%	53.0%
Religious Education Qualifications :				
Formal	66.0%	43.0%	35.0%	56.5%
Semi-Formal	78.0%	41.1%	27.0%	48.0%
None	61.0%	37.0%	20.0%	39.0%
School Type:				
Secondary	79.0%	45.0%	28.0%	50.0%
Community Comprehensive	55.0%	28.0%	25.0%	41.0%
V.E.C. Community	57.0%	38.0%	27.0%	50.0%
V.E.C. Schools	51.0%	33.0%	18.0%	45.0%
Grammar Schools (N.I.)	67.0%	48.0%	51.0%	71.0%
Secondary Schools (N.I.)	60.0%	47.0%	50.0%	63.0%
Status:				
Lay teacher	62.0%	39.0%	31.0%	48.0%
Priest	76.0%	42.0%	29.0%	51.0%
Religious Brother	84.0%	40.5%	36.0%	40.5%
Religious Sister	81.0%	50.0%	29.0%	64.0%

Table 4.2 *Continued Opposite.*

Table 4.2 *Continued*

	Administration	Staff	Senior Pupils	Junior Pupils
Region:				
Dublin	68.5%	42.0%	32.0%	51.0%
Leinster (Excluding Dublin)	69.0%	43.0%	26.0%	47.0%
Munster	70.0%	38.0%	22.5%	47.0%
Connaught	78.0%	45.0%	24.0%	49.0%
Ulster (part of)	76.0%	42.0%	24.0%	39.5%
Northern Ireland	62.0%	47.0%	50.4%	64.5%
Geographical Location:				
Rural	62.0%	37.0%	26.0%	45.0%
Small town	68.0%	36.0%	28.0%	48.0%
Large town	71.5%	47.0%	35.0%	59.0%
Suburban town	69.0%	47.0%	25.0%	49.0%
City	77.0%	47.0%	40.0%	58.5%
Gender:				
Male	68.0%	39.0%	28.0%	42.0%
Female	70.0%	43.0%	32.0%	58.0%
Average	69.2%	41.8%	30.4%	51.5%

A number of salient points emerged from a reading of this table. Firstly, respondents in the youngest age category were less inclined to believe that Religious Education had a high profile among administration and staff than was the case with their older counterparts. Secondly, respondents with formal qualifications in Religious Education had a more positive view of students' perceptions of Religious Education than respondents with no formal qualifications.

Thirdly, respondents who teach in V.E.C. schools and community/comprehensive were least likely to believe that Religious Education had a high profile among all four categories listed. Conversely, respondents in secondary schools in the Republic of Ireland and grammar schools in Northern Ireland had the most positive impressions.

Fourthly, lay teachers were generally least likely to believe Religious Education had a high profile, especially compared with religious sisters' responses.

Fifthly, respondents from Northern Ireland had more positive impressions of their pupils' views of Religious Education than did their counterparts in the Republic of Ireland. Sixthly, respondents in city schools believed Religious Education had a generally higher profile among staff and pupils than did respondents in rural schools.

Respondents listed a variety of reasons for the status of Religious Education in the school among each of the four groups mentioned above. In the case of administration, for example, the list below shows that the largest number (N=143) of respondents perceived this group to be helpful and supportive; a similar number (N=114) believed that Religious Education was an important priority for administration.

"Helpful/supportive" (mentioned by 143 respondents)
"Perceived as Important" (114)
"Good timetabling" (82)
"Disinterested/Unsupportive" (79)
"Provides facilities/resources" (62)
"Religious-run school" (60)
"Accommodate religious services" (36)
"Examination subjects are more important" (30)
"Bad timetabling" (28)
"No facilities/resources" (24)
"Important only for appearances" (11)
"Strong religious influence in the school" (10)
"Principal teaches Religious Education" (8)

The perceived support of administration for Religious Education was summed up by one teacher who said:

"Administration here are interested, supportive and ready to help financially." (59 year old teaching sister, professionally qualified).

In describing the status of Religious Education among school staff, the largest group (N=118) of respondents claimed that Religious Education was perceived as important by this group. However, an almost equal number (N=113) of respondents felt that staff were not interested in Religious Education and a further 50 respondents stated that Religious Education was unimportant to staff. The responses which were mentioned most frequently in relation to the status of Religious Education among school staff are listed opposite:

"Perceived as important" (mentioned by 118 respondents)
"Not interested" (113)
"Helpful and supportive" (86)
"Depends on particular staff" (60)
"Unimportant" (50)
"Interested" (49)
"Poor facilities" (31)
"More interested in exams" (30)
"Many are good Catholics" (28)
"A large number participate" (23)
"Religious Education is always the subject to be sacrificed" (21)

The following comments of two teachers are typical of those who expressed negative comments regarding the status of Religious Education among school staff.

"Many staff believe it should not be a subject at all." (35 year old female lay teacher, professionally qualified).

"They are only interested in their own subject and class. Religion has little interest to them." (49 year old priest, qualifications in theology).

In a similar vein, the list below demonstrates that the largest number (N=147) of respondents believed that Religious Education was interesting and important for senior pupils. However, a significantly large group (N=128) of respondents felt that senior pupils were more interested in exams, a further 99 respondents believed that seniors were disinterested in Religious Education and 54 respondents said that seniors treated Religious Education as a 'doss' class.

"Interesting/important to them" (mentioned by 147 respondents)
"More interested in exams" (128)
"Indifferent/disinterested" (99)
"Doss class" (54)
"Irrelevant to their lives" (28)
"Only important because of Religious Education exams" (21)
"Depends on the teacher" (19)
"Interested in aspects of Religious Education" (18)
"Don't know" (18)
"Some interested; some not" (16)

The following represent a small number of the negative comments made by respondents in relation to the status of Religious Education among senior students:

"A high proportion are not interested, not practising." (59 year old teaching sister, professionally qualified).

"Religion is regarded as boring and irrelevant." (28 year old female lay teacher, professionally qualified).

"Senior pupils feel compelled to profess boredom. They have had no personal experience of God." (58 year old teaching brother, no professional qualifications).

In explaining the situation with regard to junior pupils, the highest number (N=287) of respondents stated that Religious Education was an important priority for this group. However, one hundred and twenty respondents felt juniors were not interested in this subject. The responses which were cited most frequently in relation to the status of Religious Education among junior pupils are listed below:

"Important to them" (mentioned by 287 respondents)
"Not interested" (120)
"More interested in exams" (36)
"Depends on home" (24)
"Mixed levels of interest" (24)
"Depends on teacher" (24)
"Interested in aspects" (20)
"See it as a 'doss' class" (6)
"See it as a relaxing class" (5)
"Perceived as irrelevant" (5)

One teacher made the following comment regarding the importance of Religious Education to junior students:

"Most junior pupils see religion as a subject like any other. They find it stimulating and enjoyable in general." (28 year old female lay teacher, professionally qualified).

Respondents were asked to suggest ways in which Religious Education might have a higher profile in their school. Their responses, outlined in Table 4.3 opposite, demonstrate a variety of suggestions. The suggestion which was made most frequently (15%) however, was the need for more resources for Religious Education, followed by a desire for changes in the programme (14%) and examination status (12.5%).

Table 4.3 Ways in Which Religious Education could have a Higher
           Profile in the School

	Number	% of Responses	% of Respondents
More resources	102	14.7%	32.6%
Changes to Religious Education Programme	95	13.7%	30.4%
Examination status	87	12.5%	27.8%
Motivation of staff/administration	63	9.1%	20.1%
More training for teachers	62	8.9%	19.8%
Religious services in the school	56	8.1%	17.9%
Better time-tabling	52	7.5%	16.6%
Support of priests/clergy	48	6.9%	15.3%
Value of Religious Education emphasised	41	5.9%	13.1%
Support of parents	24	3.5%	7.7%
Help from experts	16	2.3%	5.1%
Motivation of pupils	7	1.0%	2.2%
More discipline	4	0.6%	1.3%

4.3   Amount of Class Time Allocated to Religious Education
The status of Religious Education in the school was further assessed by
asking respondents to indicate the average number of hours allocated
to Religious Education (per class) in their school each week. Table 4.4
below outlines the average time allocated to junior and senior cycle
Religious Education each week.

Table 4.4 Average Time Allocated Per Class to Junior and Senior
           Cycle Religious Education Each Week

	Junior Cycle		Senior Cycle	
	Number	% of Total (N=609)	Number	% of Total (N=547)
One hour	64	10.5%	71	13.0%
Two hours	413	67.8%	359	65.6%
Three hours	127	20.9%	103	18.8%
More than Three hours	5	0.8%	14	2.6%
Total	609	100.0%	547	100.0%

A comparison of average class times allocated to Religious Education
by province suggested that pupils in schools in Ulster have less Religious Education class time than their counterparts in Dublin, Leinster,
Munster, Connaught, Northern Ireland and the Republic. A far higher
percentage of respondents from schools in Ulster reported average
Religious Education class times of one hour compared to respondents
from all other provinces. This was true for both junior and senior cycles.
In a similar vein, it was found that a higher proportion of respondents
from V.E.C. community schools and V.E.C. vocational schools reported
average Religious Education class times of one hour than did their colleagues from secondary schools in Northern Ireland, community/
comprehensive schools, Northern Ireland grammar schools and secondary schools in the Republic. This was only the case for junior cycle
classes. However, it was found that secondary schools both in the Republic and Northern Ireland and grammar schools in Northern Ireland
were three times more likely to allocate three hours or more to senior
cycle Religious Education per week than V.E.C. community, V.E.C.
vocational or community/comprehensive schools.

Respondents were also asked to indicate the number of hours of Religious Education which they personally taught each week. The findings,
presented in Tables 4.5, demonstrate that approximately equal proportions of respondents teach one to two hours per week, three to four
hours per week and five to ten hours per week. This was true for both
junior and senior cycle teachers.

Table 4.5 Number of Hours of Religious Education taught by
Respondents Each Week - Junior and Senior Cycle

	Junior Cycle		*Senior Cycle*	
	Number	% of Total (N=506)	Number	% of Total (N=482)
One - Two hours	141	27.9%	141	29.3%
Three - Four hours	126	24.9%	131	27.2%
Five - Ten hours	164	32.3%	161	33.4%
Eleven hours +	75	14.9%	49	10.0%
Total	506	100.0%	482	100.0%

It will be recalled from Chapter One that respondents with formal qualifications in Religious Education taught more hours than their unquali-

fied counterparts. Similarly, teachers in the youngest age group (under 30 years) taught more hours than those in older age groups. This was true for teachers of both junior and senior cycle Religious Education. Priests were found to teach more hours of junior cycle Religious Education than lay persons, religious brothers and religious sisters, while religious brothers taught fewer hours of senior cycle Religious Education than other categories of respondents. Respondents from both grammar schools and secondary schools in Northern Ireland taught fewer hours than their counterparts from schools in the Republic although this was the case for teachers of junior cycle only.

The vast majority (84%) of teachers were satisfied that Religious Education had sufficient periods on the junior cycle timetable. This was also the case for senior cycle teachers, where 84% of respondents commented favourably on Religious Education timetable allocation (Table 4.6).

Table 4.6   Respondents are Satisfied that Religious Education has Sufficient Periods on the Junior and Senior Cycle Timetable

| | Junior Cycle | | Senior Cycle | |
	Number	% of Total (N=625)	Number	% of Total (N=543)
Yes	526	84.2%	455	83.8%
No	74	11.8%	66	12.2%
Differs from Class to Class	25	4.0%	22	4.1%
Total	625	100.0%	543	100.0%

Respondents who had indicated either satisfaction or dissatisfaction with timetabling for junior or senior cycle Religious Education were not distinguishable by age, gender, qualifications, length of time teaching, type of school or province.

Respondents who were dissatisfied with timetabling arrangements for Religious Education or who had stated that their satisfaction differed from class to class were asked to explain why they felt this way. The response which was mentioned most frequently (66%) in relation to junior cycle pupils was clearly the need for more classes (Table 4.7).

Table 4.7   Reasons for Dissatisfaction with Religious Education
Timetabling for Junior Cycle

	Number	% of Responses	% of Respondents
Not enough classes	66	66.0%	72.5%
Makes certain items difficult to teach	13	13.0%	14.3%
Depends on class	6	6.0%	6.6%
Continuity is difficult	5	5.0%	5.5%
Need to structure timetable differently	5	5.0%	5.5%
Other	5	5.0%	5.5%

One teacher summed up her dissatisfaction as follows:

"Other subjects normally get four periods. With three, there are weeks with only one or two through Holy Days etc. This makes it difficult to fit in the programme, prayer and interesting back-up activities - something usually has to be omitted." (51 year old teaching sister, professionally qualified).

The reasons offered by senior cycle Religious Education teachers for their dissatisfaction with Religious Education timetabling were quite similar to those mentioned by junior cycle teachers. Again, the response that was mentioned most frequently (47%) centred around the need for more Religious Education classes (Table 4.8).

Table 4.8   Reasons for Dissatisfaction with Religious Education
Timetabling for Senior Cycle

	Number	% of Responses	% of Respondents
Not enough classes	47	47.0%	51.6%
Limits classes	18	18.0%	19.8%
Limited status	11	11.0%	12.1%
Depends on class	11	11.0%	12.1%
Need to structure timetable differently	6	6.0%	6.6%
Too many classes	1	1.0%	1.1%
Other	6	6.0%	6.6%

Some random comments of senior cycle teachers were as follows:

"Some classes have only one period of three-quarters of an hour. That is too short. Things become slapdash." (39 year old priest, qualifications in theology).

'Two periods are insufficient as discussion time takes up a lot and the new Living Faith Series needs more time." (28 year old female lay teacher, professionally qualified).

4.4   Opportunities for Discussion of Religious Education in the School
This section seeks to establish the extent to which Religious Education teachers have the opportunity to discuss their subject with both colleagues and parents of pupils. In relation to colleagues, the results presented in Table 4.9 indicate that the majority (85%) of respondents had at least some opportunity for discussion with fellow Religious Education teachers.

Table 4.9   Teachers Have An Opportunity to Discuss Their Subject with Other Religious Education Teachers

	Number (N=662)	% of Total
Yes	562	84.9%
No	100	15.1%
Total	662	100.0%

Respondents' age, gender, qualifications, school type or province of school did not have any effect on their opportunities for discussing their subject with other Religious Education teachers. However, religious brothers were less likely than other categories of respondents to report that such opportunities existed.

Table 4.10 overleaf shows that both informal and formal meetings provided most opportunities for discussion with other Religious Education teachers.

Table 4.10 Opportunities for Discussing Religious Education with Other Teachers

	Number	% of Responses	% of Respondents
Informal meetings	324	40.3%	58.3%
Formal meetings	313	39.0%	56.3%
Outside school	58	7.2%	10.4%
Diocesan Advisor	28	3.5%	5.0%
Regular contact	22	2.7%	4.0%
When organising religious events	20	2.5%	3.6%
Team teaching	20	2.5%	3.6%
Through Head of Department	10	1.2%	1.8%

Respondents who had no opportunities for discussing their subject with other Religious Education teachers were asked to state why this was the case. Lack of organisation comprised the largest proportion of responses (31%), followed by a failure to provide time for discussion (23%) and the lack of other qualified Religious Education teachers with whom to discuss their subject (15%). Table 4.11 outlines these responses in detail.

Table 4.11 Reasons Why Respondents have No Opportunities for Discussion with Other Religious Education Teachers

	Number	% of Responses	% of Respondents
Lack of organisation	35	31.3%	35.7%
No time allotted	26	23.2%	26.5%
No other qualified R.E. teachers	17	15.2%	17.3%
Lack of interest	12	10.7%	12.2%
School too big	9	8.0%	9.2%
Too busy	3	2.7%	3.1%
Don't know	3	2.7%	3.1%
Other	7	6.3%	7.1%

In a similar vein, respondents were asked to indicate whether or not they had talked to individual parents about the Religious Education of their children. Table 4.12 demonstrates that the majority (73%) of respondents had indeed done so.

Table 4.12 Religious Education Teachers Talked to Individual Parents

	Number	% of Total (N=677)
Yes	494	73.0%
No	183	27.0%
Total	677	100.0%

As was the case for discussion of Religious Education with colleagues, respondents' age, gender or school type was found to have no significant effects on their ability to talk to individual parents about the Religious Education of their children. However, respondents' qualifications were found to be significant: teachers with no qualifications were less likely (48.5%) than those with formal (80%) or semi-formal (72%) Religious Education qualifications to talk to parents. Similarly, lay persons (70%) and religious brothers (51%) were less likely than priests (81%) or religious sisters (84%) to have engaged in such communication. Finally, teachers from schools in Dublin (86%) or Leinster (84%) were more likely than those from schools in Connaught (76%), the Republic (69%), Munster (65%), Ulster (64%) or Northern Ireland (63%) to have discussed Religious Education with parents.

Parents meetings or Parent-Teacher meetings provided by far the majority (82%) of occasions for discussion of Religious Education between teachers and parents (Table 4.13).

Table 4.13 Occasions for Discussion of Religious Education with Parents of Pupils

	Number	% of Responses	% of Respondents
Parent-Teacher Meetings	502	81.6%	100.2%
Socially (outside school)	40	6.5%	8.0%
Concerts/Plays	31	5.0%	6.2%
Parent Courses	18	2.9%	3.6%
Home visits	15	2.4%	3.0%
Informal meetings	6	1.0%	1.2%
Other	3	0.5%	0.6%

The majority (87%) of respondents found the interchange with parents helpful to them – only 13% felt that it had been an unhelpful exercise (Table 4.14).

Table 4.14 Respondents Found the Interchange With Parents Helpful

	Number (N=491)	% of Total
Yes	430	87.4%
No	61	12.6%
Total	491	100.0%

Respondents who found the interchange with parents unhelpful could not be differentiated from those who found it helpful by age, gender, qualifications or school type.

Respondents listed a variety of reasons as to why the discussion with parents had been helpful. The following were those which were mentioned most frequently:

"Parents were interested" (mentioned by 104 respondents)
"Provided an insight into pupils" (64)
"Parents were encouraging/supportive" (56)
"Useful to discuss the Religious Education programme" (55)
"Useful to get a picture of home as regards Religious Education" (54)
"Good to get parents' views" (51)
"Good to learn about child's background" (46)
"Useful to discuss problems one might have" (28)
"Led to co-operation and understanding" (15)
"Religious Education is the duty of parents also" (12)

Respondents who had stated that the interchange with parents had been unhelpful were asked to explain why this was so. The reasons they gave are listed below:

"Parents were only interested in exams" (mentioned by 40 respon dents)
"Parents were not interested in Religious Education" (36)
"Parents only wanted to discuss their child's problems" (10)
"Parents were unaware of the situation" (8)
"Meeting was too brief" (6)
"Parents only wanted traditional catechetics" (2)

4.5   Helpfulness of Principal, Chaplain and Diocesan Advisor
to Religious Education Teachers

Respondents were asked to indicate the helpfulness of the principal, the chaplain and the diocesan advisor to Religious Education teachers. The findings presented in Table 4.15 demonstrate that the majority of respondents found all three to be helpful or very helpful to Religious Education teachers (87%, 79% and 81% respectively).

Table 4.15   Helpfulness of Principal, Chaplain, Diocesan Advisor to Religious Education Teachers

	Principal	Chaplain	Diocesan Advisor
Very Helpful	38.4% (N=240)	33.0% (N=184)	27.5% (N=147)
Helpful	48.3% (N=302)	46.1% (N=257)	53.6% (N=287)
Unco-operative	2.7% (N=17)	6.5% (N=36)	4.7% (N=25)
Uninterested	10.6% (N=65)	14.4% (N=80)	14.2% (N=75)
Total	100% (N=624)	100% (N=557)	100% (N=534)

Respondents who found either the principal, the chaplain or the diocesan advisor to have been unhelpful to them were analysed by age, gender, qualifications, number of years teaching and province of school. In relation to the principal, no distinguishing characteristics for this group were found, except in the case of qualifications, where it was found that a higher percentage (23%) of those with no qualifications than those with semi-formal (8%) or formal qualifications (14%) reported their principal to have been unhelpful. No differences in responses were found when those who reported the chaplain to have been unhelpful were analysed by the characteristics mentioned above. Finally, in the case of diocesan advisors, it was found that respondents who had expressed negative comments regarding the helpfulness of the diocesan advisor tended to be in the youngest age group (less than 31 years), to be unqualified, and based in the Dublin region. Respondents' gender or number of years teaching were not differentiating characteristics in this instance.

Respondents were asked to elaborate on the answers which they had given in relation to the principal, the chaplain and the diocesan advisor. It is interesting to note that in spite of the positive answers given by respondents regarding the helpfulness of each of the three groups mentioned above, when asked to elaborate on these replies, large numbers of respondents expressed negative comments in relation to the chaplain and the diocesan advisor. The responses which were mentioned most frequently are listed below.

Principal:
"Helpful and supportive" (mentioned by 433 respondents)
"Provides resources for Religious Education" (141)
"Helpful in some respects" (87)
"Does not interfere" (78)
"Unsupportive" (71)
"Helpful if asked" (32)
"Gives no resources to Religious Education" (22)
"Supports Christian ethos" (19)
"Has other preoccupations" (18)
"Teaches Religious Education himself/herself" (15)

Chaplain:
"Helpful and supportive" (mentioned by 272 respondents)
"Helpful in some respects" (196)
"Rare/no visits" (119)
"Unhelpful" (108)
"Helpful when needed" (45)
"Visits the school" (36)
"We have no chaplain" (36)
"I am the chaplain" (29)
"Chaplain is new" (9)
"Does not interfere" (6)
"Provides resources for Religious Education" (5)

Diocesan Advisor:
"Little or no contact" (mentioned by 179 respondents)
"Helpful and supportive" (178)
"Unhelpful" (144)
"Visits the school" (126)
"Helpful in some respects" (112)
"Good organiser" (73)
"Provides resources for Religious Education" (65)
"Don't know what his/her role is" (11)

CHAPTER FIVE

The Role of Religious Education in the Future

5.1 Introduction

This chapter examines the perceptions of teachers regarding the role and present status of Religious Education in the Irish educational system. It outlines developments which teachers might wish to see in the content of Religious Education, as for example, in relation to the possibility of examination status for Religious Education in the Republic of Ireland. It also details in-service experiences and support services which Religious Education teachers would like to receive. The chapter goes on to examine the attitudes of Religious Education teachers regarding co-operation between the school and parish, as well as suggesting ways, other than the school situation, of getting across the Christian message. The final section of the chapter reviews the role of teachers themselves in Religious Education in terms of their own faith in the classroom.

5.2 Examination Status of Religious Education

As Table 5.1 demonstrates Religious Education is a public examination in most schools in Northern Ireland. Almost three-quarters (73%) of Northern Ireland respondents said Religious Education was a public examination in their school; a further 19.5% said it was a public examination in their school in some cases.

Table 5.1   Religious Education is a Public Examination in Respondent's School In Northern Ireland

	Number	% of Total (N=128*)
Yes	93	72.7%
No	10	7.8%
In Some Cases	25	19.5%
Total	128	100.0%

* Two respondents did not answer this question.

Respondents who stated that Religious Education was an examination subject "In Some Cases" were asked to specify under what circumstances this examination took place. As the list below demonstrates, the largest number (N=10) of respondents said Religious Education was an examination subject for A-level pupils only.

"A-level pupils only" (mentioned by 10 respondents)
"Better pupils only" (7)
"G.C.S.E. pupils only" (5)
"Seniors only" (3)

The majority (81%) of Northern Ireland respondents said they were satisfied with arrangements regarding the public examination of Religious Education for junior cycle pupils. This was also the case for teachers of senior cycle pupils where 80% expressed satisfaction with existing arrangements (Table 5.2).

Table 5.2   Respondents are Satisfied with Arrangements Regarding the Public Examination of Religious Education in Junior Cycle

| | Junior Cycle | | Senior Cycle | |
	Number	% of Total (N=91*)	Number	% of Total (N=97*)
Yes	74	81.3%	78	80.4%
No	7	7.7%	9	9.3%
Unsure	10	11.0%	10	10.3%
Total	91	100.0%	97	100.0%

* Note: In the case of junior cycle, 39 respondents did not reply to the question while 33 respondents did not reply in the case of senior cycle.

Respondents who had expressed satisfaction with the arrangements provided for examinations at junior cycle comprised a higher proportion of respondents with formal Religious Education qualifications (86%) than was the case for those with semi-formal qualifications (78%) or those without any Religious Education qualifications (65%). A similar trend was also evident in relation to the overall level of satisfaction with senior cycle examination arrangements where respondents with formal qualifications were more likely (84%) to express satisfaction with examination arrangements than those with semi-formal (57%) or no formal qualifications (76.5%). Other personal characteristics did not have a significant impact on respondents' answers to this question.

Respondents who had expressed dissatisfaction with examination arrangements were asked to provide alternatives to these arrangements. The suggestions made by these respondents in relation to both junior and senior cycle are listed below.

Alternatives for Juniors:
"State examination" (mentioned by 2 respondents)
"House examination status" (2)
"Diocesan examination" (1)
"Monthly assessment" (1)
"More resources" (1)

Alternatives for Seniors:
"Examination for interested pupils" (mentioned by 3 respondents)
"House examination status" (2)
"Examination would increase status" (2)
"State examination" (1)

Over half (51%) of the respondents were in favour of Religious Education being a Leaving Certificate/G.C.S.E. subject (Table 5.3).

Table 5.3   Religious Education Should be a Leaving Certificate / G.C.S.E. Subject

	Number (N=660)	% of Total
Yes	334	50.6%
No	158	23.9%
Unsure	168	25.5%
Total	660	100.0%

Respondents who were in favour of this proposal comprised a higher proportion of respondents with formal qualifications in Religious Education than with semi-formal or no qualifications i.e., 57%, 41% and 46% respectively. Other demographic characteristics, such as age and gender, had no impact on their responses. Geographical location, however, was quite significant in that almost twice as many respondents from Northern Ireland than the Republic of Ireland felt Religious Education should be a Leaving Certificate/G.C.S.E. subject.

Respondents listed a variety of reasons for the opinion they had given in relation to the possibility of Religious Education as a Leaving Certificate/G.C.S.E. subject. As the list below demonstrates, the largest number (N=251) of respondents felt that giving Religious Education examination status at senior cycle level would increase the motivation of pupils; a further 200 respondents felt it would increase the status of Religious Education as a subject, while 174 respondents commented that it would increase the knowledge of pupils. Conversely, however, 119 respondents believed that the introduction of an examination in senior cycle Religious Education would destroy its faith dimension.

"Would increase the motivation of pupils" (mentioned by 251 respondents)
"Would increase the status of Religious Education" (200)
"Would increase the knowledge of pupils" (174)
"Would destroy the faith dimension of Religious Education" (119)
"Examinations are restrictive" (44)
"Already too many examinations" (41)
"People would be only too interested in results" (40)
"Might become too academic" (40)
"Religious Education would become just another subject" (40)
"Would provide a structure for teaching Religious Education" (39)
"Religious Education is for life, not examinations" (37)
"Cannot measure a Christian in an examination" (34)
"Religious Education is not suitable for an examination" (34)
"Should be optional" (33)
"Would make life easier for Religious Education teachers" (23)

When asked to consider the notion of making Religious Education an examination subject at Junior Certificate level, only just over one-third (34%) of respondents felt this should be the case (Table 5.4). This group of respondents comprised a higher proportion of respondents with formal Religious Education qualifications than with semi-formal or no qualification i.e., 37%, 30% and 29% respectively. No other significant sub-group differences were evident.

Table 5.4   Religious Education Should be an Examination Subject at Junior Certificate Level

	Number	% of Total (N=621)
Yes	210	33.8%
No	236	38.0%
Unsure	175	28.2%
Total	621	100.0%

Respondents provided a number of explanations as to why they felt Religious Education should/should not be a subject at Junior Certificate level. The largest proportion (N=128) of respondents felt that giving examination status to junior level Religious Education would increase the motivation of students, 116 respondents felt it would increase the knowledge of pupils, while 107 respondents believed it would increase the status of Religious Education as a subject. On the other hand, 85 respondents believed that the introduction of an examination at this level would be a restriction on what they could teach. The responses in relation to this question are listed below.

"Would increase the motivation of pupils" (mentioned by 128 respondents)
"Would increase the knowledge of pupils" (116)
"Would increase the status of Religious Education" (107)
"Examinations are restrictive" (85)
"Might become too academic" (65)
"System is already too centered around examinations" (54)
"Would provide a structure for teaching Religious Education" (47)
"Religious Education would become just another subject" (44)
"No need for an examination at this level" (32)
"Would omit the personal element in Religious Education" (31)
"Would destroy the faith dimension of Religious Education" (30)
"People would only be interested in results" (25)
"There would be no love for the subject" (25)
"Cannot measure a Christian in an examination" (24)
"Religious Education is for life, not examinations" (21)

The perceived importance of faith in the teaching of Religious Education was also evident in the responses to a question which asked respondents to describe what effect they would like Religious Education to have on their pupils' personal, spiritual, work and adult life generally. Almost half the responses (48.5%) stressed the spiritual dimension of their pupils' lives, while most of the others mentioned more 'human' aspects of their lives. Their answers to this question are given below:

Desired Impact of Religious Education on Pupils' Lives:

"Encourage responsibility and personal development" (mentioned by 314 respondents)
"Assist spiritual development" (293)
"Promote a Christian way of life" (274)
"Instill a love of God" (187)
"Promote a concern for others" (171)
"Instill a sense of values" (127)
"Help them understand God" (52)
"Help them form good relations" (38)

"Facilitate appreciation of the Sacraments" (35)
"Preparation for life" (32)
"Support" (31)
"Help them enjoy life" (25)
"Pass on the faith" (10)

    5.3   Alternative Ways of Getting Across the Christian Message
Respondents were asked whether they believed that there were effective ways, other than the school situation, of getting across the Christian message. The results presented in the table below indicate that an overwhelming majority of both junior (93%) and senior cycle teachers (94.5%) believe that such alternative methods exist.

Table 5.5   Respondents Believe Other Effective Ways of Getting Across the Christian Message Exist

	Yes	No	Don't Know	Total
Juniors	92.9%	7.1%	--	100%
	(N=444)	(N=34)	--	(N=478)
Seniors	94.5%	5.3%	0.2%	100%
	(N=426)	(N=24)	(N=1)	(N=451)

Respondents outlined a variety of alternative ways for getting across the Christian message. The list below outlines those mentioned most frequently in relation to junior cycle pupils:

"The home/parents" (mentioned by 125 respondents)
"The parish/local community" (123)
"The Church/priests" (101)
"Extra-curricular activities" (74)
"Clubs/societies" (69)
"Youth clubs" (62)
"Retreats" (61)
"Social work" (53)
"Example of others" (51)
"Prayer meetings" (44)
"Group work" (21)
"Media" (16)
"Parish ministries" (10)

The following are those ways of communicating the Christian message which were mentioned most frequently by teachers of senior cycle pupils:

"The parish/local community" (mentioned by 137 respondents)
"Clubs/societies" (132)
"The home/parents" (94)
"Retreats" (86)
"Example of others" (83)
"The Church/priests" (79)
"Extra-curricular activities" (61)
"Social work" (61)
"Prayer meetings" (44)
"Folk group/choir" (29)
"Study groups" (19)
"Media" (19)
"Group work" (14)
"Parish ministries" (13)

5.4   Role of Teachers' Faith in the Classroom

Respondents were asked to comment on the importance of their own faith in fostering faith in the classroom. The majority (95%) of teachers, as Table 5.6 clearly demonstrates, believe their own faith to be an important component in teaching Religious Education.

Table 5.6   Respondents' Agreement with the Suggestion that a Teacher's Own Faith is a Vital Component in Fostering Faith in the Classroom

	Number	% of Total (N=665)
Strongly Agree	494	74.3%
Agree	139	20.9%
Unsure	26	3.9%
Disagree	3	0.5%
Strongly Disagree	3	0.5%
Total	665	100.0%

Respondents who agreed with the suggestion that a teacher's own faith is "a vital component in fostering faith in the classroom" offered a number of reasons as to why they felt this was the case.

The list below outlines these responses in detail:

"Cannot teach Religious Education without faith" (mentioned by 379 respondents)
"Pupils see through teachers' lack of faith" (159)
"Pupils need to see example/faith lived out" (151)
"Religion is caught not taught" (43)
"Hypocritical if no faith" (23)
"Without faith, Religious Education is just empty words" (14)

By far the largest number of respondents (N=379) felt that Religious Education would be impossible to teach without faith. The following comments of two teachers adequately express the sentiments of those who felt this way:

"If you are not committed yourself there is no way you can find meaning or reward or in any way enhance the faith of the pupils." (29 year old female lay teacher, professionally qualified).

"Teaching Religious Education is not just teaching knowledge even though that is an important part. Belief and practice are also transmitted. A teacher's own convictions are implicitly relayed to the pupils. It is impossible to be convincing about something one does not endeavour to put into practice." (50 year old teaching sister, professionally qualified).

One hundred and fifty nine respondents believed that pupils see through a teacher's lack of faith. One teacher commented as follows:

"Kids can easily detect when you are serious or genuine." (24 year old female lay teacher, professionally qualified).

A similar number of respondents (N=151) felt that faith is only passed on through example of others or through seeing others live out their faith.

"To foster faith in the classroom you must give enthusiasm and be enthusiastic. You must be willing to live as a Christian in the class – to forgive and be forgiven, to love even those you don't like in class, to keep starting again." (28 year old priest, qualifications in theology).

Respondents who disagreed or were unsure of the value of a teacher's own faith in fostering faith in the classroom also provided explanations for their opinions. The largest number (N=27) of this group felt that influences, other than the teacher, were more important for the passing on of faith. The following comments of two teachers illustrate this point of view:

"If faith is not fostered in the home, a teacher has little chance of success." (43 year old female lay teacher, no formal qualifications).

"A teacher's example is only second to the example of parents. If parental example is less than satisfactory, it is almost impossible to instill a value for Christian attitudes in the child." (35 year old male lay teacher, no formal qualifications).

A similar number of respondents (N=22) believed that the possession of faith was not necessary for teaching Religious Education. This feeling was summed up by one teacher as follows:

"Even though I myself have faith, it is I believe, nevertheless possible to teach religion and not believe in anything. A good teacher is a good teacher. For example - an English teacher doesn't have to believe that Jane Austen was a great writer in order to present her to a class." (27 year old female lay teacher, no formal qualifications).

Other comments made by these respondents include: "Doubt is an important part of teaching" (mentioned by 8 respondents) and "Knowledge is more important than teachers' faith" (4).

Respondents were also asked to comment on the suggestion that "Religion is caught not taught". More than two-thirds (67%) of respondents believed this statement to be true for teaching Religious Education; 13% disagree with the statement and 20% were unsure (Table 5.7). Respondents who disagreed with the suggestion did not differ from the total group of respondents in any significant way.

Table 5.7   Respondents' Agreement with the Suggestion that Religion is Caught not Taught

	Number	% of Total (N=636)
Strongly Agree	215	33.8%
Agree	212	33.3%
Unsure	125	19.7%
Disagree	69	10.8%
Strongly Disagree	15	2.4%
Total	636	100.0%

Among those respondents who agreed with the statement, the largest number (N=195) felt that pupils acquired faith through the example of others, i.e., seeing others live out their faith:

"All the technique in the world cannot replace the solid at ease attitude of the teacher." (57 year old teaching brother, no formal qualifications).

"Relationship with students is essential - people generally acquire the values of those whom they perceive as wholesome. Teachers and students must respect each other's dignity. It should be evolved and fostered as opposed to hammered." (28 year old female lay teacher, professionally qualified).

Ninety-seven respondents believed that religion is caught in the home. The following comment of one teacher sums up this attitude:

"Religion is, for the most part, caught in the home and school can have little impact if this does not happen in the home." (42 year old male lay teacher, professionally qualified).

Other comments made by those who believed that religion is caught rather than taught included: "Pupils see through a teacher who lacks faith" (mentioned by 9 respondents); and "A teacher needs to believe" (7).

One hundred and sixty-eight respondents felt that the statement was not wholly true and that religion was both caught and taught. The comments below are representative of those who held this view:

"I feel it [Religion] is both caught and taught. They will not follow our example unless we can teach them why all this is important to us." (28 year old female lay teacher, professionally qualified).

"I have heard this so often that now I'm not sure. I do believe a Godly/ religious atmosphere in the home and neighbourhood is essential in fostering religious growth; but there is definitely a lot to be said for some knowledge to help one's own faith/conviction grow." (43 year old male lay teacher, no formal qualifications).

Other comments made by respondents who had expressed uncertainty or who disagreed with the suggestion that "Religion is caught, not taught" include: "Teaching is more important" (mentioned by 38 respondents); "Influences other than the teacher are more important for the pupils" (35); "Knowledge is important to back up faith" (30); "Faith is caught, Religious Education is taught" (29); and "What pupils learn in class may be all the Religion they get" (8). Some random comments of these respondents are as follows:

"The faith has to be caught but a well structured class can ensure attitudes, values, information are learned even if the teacher has little personal faith." (24 year old female lay teacher, professionally qualified).

"I think that a statement like that can be too elusive. If you don't have something to be taught, then why go in and teach. There must be a body of information to be put across apart from all the other stuff that we must do with the young people." (28 year old priest, qualifications in theology).

"I believe that the moment a child asks why about the wonder of life and receives an answer, thus begins the teaching of Religion. You can catch Religion for a while but it will wither without a solid background of knowledge and understanding to inspire that faith." (29 year old female lay teacher, professionally qualified).

5.5   Co-operation Between School and Parish

Table 5.8 below demonstrates that the vast majority (89%) of respondents would like to see co-operation between their school and the wider parish in teaching Religious Education.

Table 5.8   Respondents Would Like to See Greater Co-operation Between School and Parish

	Number	% of Total (N=592)
Yes	529	89.4%
No	63	10.6%
Total	592	100.0%

Respondents who expressed a desire for such co-operation offered a number of explanations for their opinion. As the list below demonstrates, the largest number (N=154) of respondents simply felt that school and parish should be linked in some way. Eighty-seven respondents would like to see greater involvement of the clergy in the schools, while 58 respondents believed that there should be greater co-operation between the school and parents of pupils.

"Parish and school should be linked" (mentioned by 154 respondents)
"Clergy should be involved more" (87)
"Parents and school should be working together" (58)
"Would like co-operation but not realistic" (55)
"Should be greater co-operation in Church services" (50)
"Pupils should be involved in the parish" (40)
"School, home and parish should be linked" (37)

"School and parish should be linked but with certain conditions" (20)
"School is already involved with the parish" (22)
"Clergy are not interested" (17)

Some of the comments made by these respondents include the following:

"It would be so encouraging if the local clergy and parish would show any interest in co-operating with school events - at least our students would see some continuity and meeting of interests." (26 year old female lay teacher, professionally qualified).

"I see this [co-operation between school and wider community] as essential. Parents, teachers, clergy, parishioners, could ideally be involved in passing on the Christian message - no group can do it alone in to-day's society." (49 year old teaching sister, professionally qualified).

Of those respondents who did not wish for co-operation between the school and the wider community in teaching Religious Education, the largest number (N=34) felt that such co-operation was not realistically possible. This was summed up by one respondents as follows:

"Co-operation like that is not possible as the pupils come from such a variety of parishes." (51 year old teaching sister, no formal qualifications).

Respondents who had already co-operated with the parish in teaching Religious Education were asked to indicate their level of satisfaction with this activity - just over half (54%) of these respondents expressed some level of satisfaction; 19.5% expressed dissatisfaction, while a further 26.5% stated that they had mixed feelings (Table 5.9).

Table 5.9   Degree of Satisfaction Experienced by Respondents in Their Co-operation with Parish

	Number	% of Total (N=226)
Very Satisfied	44	19.5%
Satisfied	78	34.5%
Mixed Feelings	60	26.5%
Not Satisfied	28	12.4%
Totally Dissatisfied	16	7.1%
Total	226	100.0%

Respondents who had experienced satisfaction in their dealings with the parish were asked to explain why they felt this way. As the list below demonstrates, the largest number (N=24) indicated that they had been satisfied with their involvement in Church services and/or Sacraments; 16 respondents indicated that they had co-operated satisfactorily with the priests in their parish, while 11 respondents said that they had experienced a good community spirit.

"Satisfied with involvement in Church services/Sacraments" (mentioned by 24 respondents)
"Satisfied with co-operation with priests of parish" (16)
"Good community spirit" (11)
"Satisfied with co-operation" (11)
"Satisfied with meetings in parish" (8)
"Satisfied with social work involvement in parish" (6)
"Satisfied with involvement in parish groups" (2)
"Made links with other schools possible" (2)
"Of value to pupils" (2)
"Satisfied with involvement in parish youth work" (1)

Respondents who had mixed feelings or who had experienced dissatisfaction in their co-operation with the parish made a number of complaints. The following are those which were mentioned most frequently.

"Priests were unco-operative" (mentioned by 29 respondents)
"Little or no co-operation was given" (14)
"Involvement in Church services/Sacraments was dissatisfactory" (10)
"Co-operation was insufficient" (7)
"Co-operation was not possible" (6)
"Insufficient numbers were involved" (4)

One teacher summed up his dissatisfaction as follows:

"We offer adult Religious Education each year to the parents/guardians of our pupils – twenty approximately take up the offer." (38 year old male lay teacher, professionally qualified).

   5.6   *Support Services Desired by Religious Education Teachers*
Respondents were asked to indicate how well prepared they felt to teach Religious Education. The table overleaf demonstrates that just over one-quarter (26%) of respondents considered themselves to be well prepared, 51.5% regarded themselves to be adequately prepared while 22% felt they were poorly prepared or not prepared at all to teach Religious Education.

Table 5.10 How Well Prepared Respondents Feel to Teach Religion

	Number	% of Total (N=662)
Well Prepared	174	26.3%
Adequately Prepared	341	51.5%
Poorly Prepared	123	18.6%
Not Prepared At All	24	3.6%
Total	662	100.0%

Respondents who felt "Poorly Prepared" or "Not Prepared At All" comprised a higher proportion of respondents with no formal qualifications for teaching Religious Education (60%) than their counterparts with semi-formal (21%) or formal (12%) qualifications. Other demographic characteristics did not have a significant impact on their answers to this question.

Respondents mentioned a variety of in-service experiences which would be of assistance to them in teaching Religious Education. The list below shows that the largest proportion (N=172) of respondents would like help in the area of methodology, 79 respondents perceived the need for additional resources, while 72 respondents would like the opportunity to meet with their colleagues.

"Training in methodology" (mentioned by 172 respondents)
"Resources" (79)
"Meet other Religious Education teachers" (72)
"Religious services" (59)
"Information on the syllabus" (57)
"Courses" (54)
"Information on the Gospels" (54)
"Information on Theology/Church teachings" (39)
"Information on youth" (34)
"Information on the Sacraments" (31)
"Information on social problems" (31)
"Information on sexuality" (31)
"Training in group work" (31)
"Training in teaching Religious Education to remedial pupils" (27)
"An increase in faith" (22)
"Outside support" (19)
"Training in the use of dance/drama/music in Religious Education" (19)

In a similar vein, respondents were asked to indicate other support services which would be of assistance to them in teaching Religious Education. The largest number (N=124) of respondents indicated a desire for more resources; a similar number (N=108) mentioned a need for support from the clergy; 80 respondents expressed a desire for meeting other Religious Education teachers. These and other responses made by teachers are listed below:

"Additional resources" (mentioned by 124 respondents)
"Support from clergy/chaplain" (108)
"Meet with other Religious Education teachers" (80)
"Videos" (76)
"Support from parish/parents" (67)
"Resource centre" (52)
"Better texts" (43)
"Better diocesan advisor service" (43)
"Information on guest speakers" (36)
"Religious services in the school" (35)
"Courses" (29)
"Audio visual aids" (22)
"Experts to advise" (21)
"Religion room" (18)
"Information on available material" (15)
"List for retreat work" (14)

National Profile
of Religious Education Teachers

The information presented in this appendix is drawn from a national profile of 4,565 Religious Education teachers based in 773 Catholic post-primary schools throughout Northern Ireland and the Republic of Ireland.* This figure represents 85% of the total number of all Catholic post-primary schools in Ireland; the remaining 15% of schools did not return questionnaires. The data was compiled by the staff of the Council for Research and Development in conjunction with post-primary diocesan advisors and school principals.

1.1   Location of Schools in Which Teachers are Based
Respondents were drawn from schools in the twenty-six dioceses of Ireland. Details of the number of schools from each diocese are listed in Appendix Table 1.

Table 1 Distribution of Schools by Ecclesiastical Province and Diocese

Diocese	Number	% of Total (N=761*)
Province of Armagh:		
Armagh	31	4.1%
Ardagh and Clonmacnoise	16	2.1%
Clogher	16	2.1%
Derry	23	3.0%
Down and Connor	42	5.5%
Dromore	7	0.9%
Kilmore	14	1.8%
Meath	36	4.7%
Raphoe	14	1.8%
Province of Dublin:		
Dublin	195	25.6%
Ferns	14	1.8%
Kildare and Leighlin	47	6.2%
Ossory	19	2.5%

Table 1 *Continued Opposite.*

Table 1 *Continued*

Diocese	Number	% of Total (N=761*)
Province of Cashel:		
Cashel and Emly	26	3.4%
Cloyne	33	4.3%
Cork and Ross	41	5.4%
Kerry	31	4.1%
Killaloe	27	3.5%
Limerick	35	4.6%
Waterford and Lismore	18	2.4%
Province of Tuam:		
Tuam	14	1.8%
Achonry	9	1.2%
Clonfert	8	1.1%
Elphin	19	2.5%
Galway	14	1.8%
Killala	12	1.6%
Total	761	100.0%

* Twelve schools did not indicate their diocese

Appendix Table 2 overleaf details participating schools by county.

* The total number of post-primary schools in the Republic of Ireland in 1988 was 814. The twenty-two Protestant secondary schools, the five state comprehensive/community schools under Protestant management, and the one Jewish school were not included in the present research. In addition, the questionnaires were sent to 119 Catholic-run schools in Northern Ireland. Accordingly, the total number of Catholic post-primary schools in Ireland is 905.

Table 2 Distribution of Schools by County

County	Number	% of Total (N=773)
Armagh	7	0.9%
Antrim	34	4.4%
Down	15	1.9%
Derry	18	2.3%
Fermanagh	9	1.2%
Tyrone	16	2.1%
Monaghan	7	0.9%
Cavan	9	1.2%
Donegal	16	2.1%
Cork	82	10.6%
Kerry	33	4.3%
Clare	19	2.5%
Limerick	41	5.3%
Waterford	15	1.9%
Tipperary	33	4.3%
Louth	15	1.9%
Laois	18	2.3%
Offaly	14	1.8%
Carlow	9	1.2%
Kilkenny	15	1.9%
Wexford	15	1.9%
Kildare	28	3.6%
Longford	6	0.8%
Westmeath	13	1.7%
Meath	16	2.1%
Dublin	168	21.7%
Wicklow	19	2.5%
Sligo	13	1.7%
Roscommon	11	1.4%
Galway	27	3.5%
Leitrim	8	1.0%
Mayo	24	3.1%
Total	773	100.0%

The distribution of all Catholic schools in the Republic of Ireland and those schools which participated in the project are listed in Appendix Table 3. Not included in this table are the 100 Catholic schools in Northern Ireland who also took part (Appendix Table 4).

Table 3 Distribution of Schools in the Republic of Ireland

Region	Actual Distribution		National Profile	
	No.	%	No.	%
Dublin	184	23.3%	168	24.9%
Leinster (excluding Dublin)	188	23.9%	168	24.9%
Munster	251	31.9%	223	33.0%
Connaught	123	15.6%	83	12.3%
Ulster (part of)	42	5.3%	32	4.7%
Total	788	100.0%	674	100.0%

Source: The actual distribution of schools by state and region was derived from data compiled by the Department of Education.

The results presented in Appendix Table 3 above indicate that the distribution of schools in the national profile, comprised of 85% of all Catholic schools in Ireland, is very close to the complete distribution of schools.

1.2   Characteristics of Schools in Which Teachers are Based

The majority of Religious Education teachers who were included in this national profile taught in secondary schools either in the Republic of Ireland (52.5%) or in Northern Ireland (10%); a further 27% taught in V.E.C. schools. Details of school type are provided in Appendix Table 4 below.

Table 4 Distribution of Schools by Type of School

Type of School	Number	% of Total (N=771)
Republic of Ireland:		
Secondary Voluntary School	405	52.5%
V.E.C.	206	26.7%
Community	49	6.4%
Comprehensive	11	1.4%
Northern Ireland:		
Grammar School	24	3.1%
Secondary School	76	9.9%
Total	771	100.0%

The largest percentage (45%) of schools in the profile were schools with both male and female pupils; 27% were all-girls' schools and 24% were restricted to boys only.

Schools in the sample were of varying sizes as indicated in Appendix Table 5.

Table 5 Distribution of Schools by Size of School

Number of Pupils	Number	% of Total (N=726*)
100 pupils or less	23	3.2%
101 - 200 pupils	84	11.6%
201 - 300 pupils	131	18.0%
301 - 400 pupils	118	16.3%
401 - 500 pupils	101	13.9%
501 - 600 pupils	99	13.6%
601 - 700 pupils	63	8.7%
701 - 800 pupils	48	6.6%
801 - 900 pupils	32	4.4%
Over 900 pupils	27	3.7%
Total	726	100.0%

* No details were provided for 47 schools

1.3 Characteristics of Religious Education Teachers

Schools were asked to specify the gender and status (i.e. lay person, priest, religious brother, religious sister) of their Religious Education teachers. The majority (58%) of teachers included in the profile were female; 42% were male. Most (71%) were lay persons; 29% were religious personnel. In relation to male respondents, 68% were lay teachers, 22% were religious brothers and 10% were priests. A breakdown of Religious Education teachers according to their status is provided in Appendix Table 6.

Table 6 Status of Religious Education Teachers

Status	Number	% of Total (N=4565)
Lay Person	3,235	70.9%
Priest	421	9.2%
Religious Brother	198	4.3%
Religious Sister	711	15.6%
Total	4,565	100.0%

The results presented in Appendix Table 7 show that less than half (44%) of all Religious Education teachers in the profile possessed catechetical qualifications. However, it must be stressed that this does not mean that only 44% of students are taught by qualified teachers. Rather, as shown in Chapter One of the Report, Religious Education teachers with formal qualifications teach more Religious Education hours than their unqualified counterparts.

Table 7 Religious Education Teachers have Catechetical Qualifications

	Number	% of Total (N=4,560*)
Yes	2,025	44.4%
No	2,005	44.0%
No Response	530	11.6%
Total	4,560	100.0%

*This information was not provided for five R. E. teachers

Appendix Table 8 demonstrates that the highest percentage (39%) of Religious Education teachers taught junior level, 28% taught a combination of senior and junior; 24% taught senior only.

Table 8 Class Level Taught

Class Level	Number	% of Total (N=4,565)
Junior	1,775	38.9%
Senior and Junior	1,289	28.3%
Senior	1,084	23.8%
No Information	417	9.0%
Total	4,565	100.0%

1.4 Summary of National Profile

Religious Education teachers in this profile were drawn from 26 dioceses throughout Ireland: all counties and provinces were represented in the profile. Secondary schools in both the Republic and Northern Ireland represented the majority (79%) of schools in the profile. Schools were found to be of varying sizes; the largest percentage (45%) were mixed schools.

The majority of Religious Education teachers were female; most (71%) were lay persons; less than half (44%) had catechetical qualifications. The highest percentage (39%) of Religious Education teachers taught junior level classes.

Council for Research & Development

April 1989

Dear R.E. Teacher,

The Council for Research and Development have been requested by the Episcopal Commission for Catechetics and the Catechetical Association of Ireland to carry out a national survey of Religious Education teachers' opinions of their task as teachers of religion. It is hoped that the results of this survey will highlight the needs and attitudes of R.E. teachers at post-primary level in Ireland and lead to changes which will be of benefit both to teachers and students alike.

In order to establish an accurate and representative picture of the current situation in Ireland, we require a random sample of approximately 1,200 teachers in more than 500 schools throughout the country. Your name was randomly selected from the total list of R.E. teachers in these schools and I would be very grateful if you would complete the enclosed questionnaire. **YOUR ANSWERS WILL BE TREATED WITH THE STRICT-EST CONFIDENCE AND AT NO TIME WILL ANY PERSON, OTHER THAN OUR STAFF, SEE YOUR INDIVIDUAL COMMENTS.**

The questions were designed with the assistance of experienced R.E. teachers who were also chosen at random from various schools throughout Ireland. However, if, for whatever reason, you would prefer not to answer all of the questions, please use your own discretion. I would like to stress that in the interests of establishing an accurate picture of the overall situation, I hope that most of you will be in a position to answer all of the questions, even if you feel you have nothing special to say.

Finally, a note to those of you who would prefer not to participate in this research project. Please return the enclosed questionnaire, stating why you are not interested.

Thank you for your assistance in this important survey. Since its success and eventual usefulness depend entirely on your co-operation, I would urge you to complete the enclosed, confidential questionnaire and return it in the enclosed pre-paid envelope as soon as possible.

With best wishes,

Yours sincerely,

John A. Weafer.
(Director)

ST. PATRICK'S COLLEGE ● MAYNOOTH ● CO. KILDARE ● IRELAND
TELEPHONE 01● 285418/285222

STRICTLY CONFIDENTIAL

R.E. TEACHERS' QUESTIONNAIRE

1(a)   Do you use R.E. texts regularly?

                Yes..........1   No...........2
                    (Please circle one number)

        [If NO, skip to Q.1 (f), page 3]

   (b)   If YES, please indicate the major R.E. text or series
         used by you in your various classes:

                        Text/Series

        1st. YEAR:_____

        2nd. YEAR:_____

        3rd. YEAR:_____

        4th. YEAR:_____

        5th. YEAR:_____

        6th. YEAR:_____

        Other (Specify): _____

   (c)   In general, how useful do you find these texts in
         teaching R.E.? (Please indicate the text/series to
         which your comments apply and circle one number on
         each line).

Text/Series	Very Useful	Useful	Sometimes Useful	Not Useful	Totally Useless
_____	1	2	3	4	5
_____	1	2	3	4	5
_____	1	2	3	4	5
_____	1	2	3	4	5
_____	1	2	3	4	5
_____	1	2	3	4	5
_____	1	2	3	4	5

NOTE: If you require additional space to answer any question(s), please do so
        on a separate page and indicate the question number to which the
        information applies.

2

(d)   Please list those parts of the texts/series which you
       find MOST USEFUL. (Please be as specific as possible).

Text/Series	Most Useful Characteristics

(e)   Please list those parts of the texts/series which you
       find LEAST USEFUL.   (Please be as specific as
       possible).

Text/Series	Least Useful Characteristics

(f)   If NO to Q. 1(a), please (i) specify what you use
        instead of R.E. texts, and (ii) explain why you do
        not use R.E. Texts.

        (i)_____

        _____

        _____

        _____

        _____

        _____

        _____

        (ii)_____

        _____

        _____

        _____

        _____

        _____

        _____

        _____

        _____

4

2(a)   Do you use other resource materials when teaching
       R.E.? (i.e., apart from the R.E. texts). (Please
       circle one number).

                    Yes........1   No..........2

(b)   If YES to Q.2(a), please indicate which of the
       following resource materials you use and the frequency
       of their use. (Please indicate cycle and stream if the
       resource is specific to either).

Resource Materials	Cycle (Junior/ Senior)	Stream (Lower/ Upper)	Frequency of Use (Frequently/Some- times/Rarely/Never)
Video			
Guest Speakers			
Field Work			
Discussion			
Prayer/Meditation			
Audio tapes/ records			
Magazines			
Bible			
Experiential activities			
Role Play			
Other (Specify):			

3(a)   Have you used the Christian Way series? (Please circle
       one number on each line)

	YES	NO
Christian Way I	1	2
Christian Way II	1	2
Christian Way III	1	2
Come Follow Me	1	2

5

(b) How would you rate this series? (Please circle one number on each line).

	Excellent	Good	Average	Poor
TEACHERS' BOOK				
Christian Way I	1	2	3	4
Christian Way II	1	2	3	4
Christian Way III	1	2	3	4
Come Follow Me	1	2	3	4
STUDENTS' BOOK				
Christian Way I	1	2	3	4
Christian Way II	1	2	3	4
Christian Way III	1	2	3	4
Come Follow Me	1	2	3	4

(c) If this series (Christian Way I, II, III) were presented again, should it be the same or different? (Please circle one number).

    Same............1   Different........2

Please elaborate: _____

_____

_____

4(a) Do you find the following persons helpful to you, as a teacher of R.E.? (Please circle one number on each line).

	Very Helpful	Helpful	Unco-op erative	Unint- erested
Principal:	1	2	3	4
Chaplain:	1	2	3	4
Diocesan Advisor:	1	2	3	4

6

(b)   Please elaborate on your answers to Question 4(a):

        Principal: _____

        _____

        _____

        Chaplain: _____

        _____

        _____

        Diocesan Advisor:_____

        _____

        _____

5(a)   Have you talked to individual parents about the
        religious education of their children?

                Yes............1   No.............2

   (b) If YES,
        - On what occasion(s) did you do so?_____

        _____

        - Did you find the interchange helpful?   Yes........1

                                                  No.........2

        - If YES, please explain: _____

        _____

        - If NO, please indicate why not: _____

        _____

7

6.   IN GENERAL, (given that there may be many differences
(a)   between classes), which of the following phrases best
      describes your experience of teaching R.E.? (Please
      identify, in order of priority (1,2,3) the
      descriptions which come closest to your experience.

      -    It's a rewarding experience.................(___)

      -    It's a challenging but rewarding experience..(___)

      -    Alright, but difficult at times.............(___)

      -    I just manage to get through it.............(___)

      -    I find it very difficult....................(___)

      -    I wish I could give it up...................(___)

      -    Other (specify)............................(___)

      _____

(b)   Please   develop the item which received highest
      priority (No. 1) in 6(a) above:

      _____

      _____

      _____

      _____

      _____

      _____

7.(a) Does the above experience vary from class to class?

            Yes...........1   No............2

  (b) If YES, please explain why _____

      _____

      _____

8

8.   Why do you continue to teach RE? (Please indicate, in
        order of priority (1,2,3) those statements which come
        closest to your opinion).

        - It's a career, like any other..............(____)

        - Personal interest in teaching generally....(____)

        - Personal interest in teaching R.E..........(____)

        - I am not trained for anything else.........(____)

        - I am obliged to teach RE by my Principal...(____)

        - Don't Know.................................(____)

        - Other (Specify)............................(____)

        _____(____)

        _____(____)

9(a)   What other subjects do you teach at present?

        _____

        _____

(b)   In general, do you find teaching RE more or less
        satisfying than teaching other subjects?

                        More satisfying........1
                        About the same.........2
                        Less satisfying........3
                        Don't Know.............4

(c)   Have you ever seriously considered giving up teaching
        R.E.?
                        Yes..........1   No............2

        Please elaborate:_____   ___

        _____

        _____

        _____

9

10.   Has your motivation for teaching R.E. changed over the
        years?

                Yes............1   No.............2

        If YES, please (a) indicate how your motivation has
        changed and (b) give reason(s) as to why it has
        changed.

        _____

        _____

        _____

        _____

        _____

11.   Recall ONE worthwhile religion class you have taught
        and complete the following:

(a)   Year of Pupils (1st. 2nd. 3rd. etc) _____

(b)   Ability of pupils (High, medium, low, mixed)_____

(c)   Subject of the lesson   _____

(d)   Method of teaching: (Please circle appropriate item(s))

        Book   Audio   Visual   Experiential   Other

         1   2   3   4   5

        If OTHER, please specify:_____

        _____

(e)   Why did you think the class was worthwhile for the
        PUPILS?

        _____

        _____

        _____

(f)   Why did you think it was worthwhile for YOU?

        _____

        _____

        _____

10

12.   What effect would you like religious education to have
       on your pupils i.e., in their personal, spiritual,
       work, and adult life generally etc.)?

_____

_____

_____

_____

_____

_____

_____

13(a) Are there any topics in R.E. which you find difficult
       to teach? (Please include topics which you avoid
       because of some difficulty).

              Yes............1   No............2

  (b) If YES, please list up to five which present most
       difficulty to you: (Please indicate year level and
       streaming level if the difficulty is specific to it).

Topic	Cycle (Junior/ Senior)	Streaming (Lower/ Upper)
1.		
2.		
3.		
4.		
5.		

11

(c)   Why do you find these topics difficult to teach?

1._____

_____

2._____

_____

3._____

_____

4._____

_____

5._____

_____

14.   Are there topics omitted from your course text(s)
        which you would like to see included? (Please circle
        one number)

                Yes..........1   No...........2

        If Yes, please list up to 3 of these topics below

                Topic   Year Level

        1._____   _____

        2._____   _____

        3._____   _____

15(a)   What is the average time allocated to RE (per class)
        in your school each week?

                Junior Cycle: _____ hours

                Senior Cycle: _____ hours

  (b)   How many hours RE do you personally teach each week?

                Junior Cycle: _____ hours

                Senior Cycle: _____ hours

12

16.   Are you satisfied that R.E. has sufficient periods on the school time-table? (Please circle one number)

	YES	NO	IT DIFFERS FROM CLASS TO CLASS
Junior Cycle:	1	2	3
Senior Cycle:	1	2	3

If "NO" or "IT DIFFERS", please explain

Junior Cycle:_____

_____

Senior Cycle:_____

_____

17(a) Is there an opportunity for you to discuss your subject with other R.E. teachers? (Please circle one number).
                    Yes........1   No........2

  (b) If Yes, please indicate what opportunities you have:

_____

_____

  (c) If No, please say why:

_____

_____

18.   Is R.E. a public examination subject within the school? (Please circle one number)

                    Yes...............1

                    No................2

                    In some cases......3 (Specify)

                    _____

                    _____

13

19.   Are you satisfied with this arrangement? (Please circle one number)

	Yes	No	Unsure
Junior Cycle:	1	2	3
Senior Cycle:	1	2	3

If NO, what alternative(s) could you suggest?

Junior Cycle:_____

_____

Senior Cycle:_____

_____

20(a) Are you in favour of R.E. being a Leaving Cert. /G.C.S.E. Subject?

Yes.........1   No..........2   Unsure........3

Please give 3 reasons (if possible) for your opinion

1._____

2._____

3._____

(b) Are you in favour of R.E. being an examination subject at Junior Certificate level?

Yes.........1   No..........2   Unsure.......3

Please give 3 reasons (if possible) for your opinion

1._____

2._____

3._____

14

21.   In general do you think that R.E. has a high profile
in the school among the following? (Please circle
numbers as appropriate).

	Yes	No	Don't Know
Administration	1	2	3
Staff	1	2	3
Pupils – Senior	1	2	3
Pupils – Junior	1	2	3

- **Please explain your opinion:**

Administration:_____

_____

Staff: _____

_____

Pupils – Senior:_____

_____

Pupils – Junior: _____

_____

22.   If NO to any Section in Q.21, please suggest 3 ways in
which R.E. might have a higher profile in your school.

1._____

_____

2._____

_____

3._____

_____

15

23(a)   How many years experience have you as a R.E. Teacher?

_____ years

(b)   Was all this in Ireland?   Yes......1 No........2

If NO, give details of teaching experience:

Location(s)   Duration   When Completed

_____

_____

_____

24.   Please indicate any FORMAL TRAINING you have received
for teaching R.E.? (include degrees/diplomas in R.E.,
theology, extra mural diplomas, inservice courses
etc.)

Formal Training	Duration of Course(s)	Year Course Completed

25.   List any R.E. inservice courses you may have done over the
last 5 years: (include courses which assist you in teaching
R.E.)

Subject of Course	Duration	Helpful (Yes/No)
_____	_____	_____
_____	_____	_____
_____	_____	_____
_____	_____	_____
_____	_____	_____

16

26.   How do you rate yourself as professionally prepared to
       teach R.E.? (Please circle appropriate number)

Well Prepared	Adequately Prepared	Poorly Prepared	Not prepared at all
1	2	3	4

27   What further INSERVICE experiences would be of
       assistance to you? Please name as many as you wish:

       1._____
       _____

       2._____
       _____

       3._____
       _____

       4._____
       _____

       5._____
       _____

28.   What other support services would be of assistance to you in
       teaching R.E? Please name as many as you wish.

       1._____
       _____

       2._____
       _____

       3._____
       _____

       4._____
       _____

       5._____
       _____

17

29. Has your experience of teaching R.E. changed over the
(a) years since you began to teach the subject?

              Yes......1   No.......2

(b) If YES, was the change for the better or worse?

              For Better   For Worse   Mixed
                  1   2   3

    Please explain briefly:_____

    _____

30(a) Apart from the school situation, are there other effective
      ways of getting across the Christian message for:

                                        Yes   No

          Juniors (14-15 years)   1   2

          Seniors (16-18 years)   1   2

(b)   Please elaborate:

      Juniors:_____

      _____

      Seniors:_____

      _____

31(a) Would you like to see co-operation between your school and
      the wider parish in teaching R.E.? (Please circle one
      number)

              Yes...........1   No.............2

      Please elaborate: _____

      _____

      _____

18

(b)   If you have already co-operated with the parish, how
      satisfied were you with this activity? (Please circle
      one number)

      Very   Satisfied   Mixed   Not   Totally
      Satisfied   Feelings   Satisfied   Dissatisfied

        1   2   3   4   5

      Please elaborate:_____

      _____

      _____

32.   Please indicate your level of agreement or
      disagreement with the following statements and, if you
      wish, comment on their accuracy from your own
      experience.

(a)   "A teacher's own faith is a vital component in
      fostering faith in the classroom"

            (Please circle one number)

         Strongly   Agree   Unsure   Disagree   Strongly
         Agree   Disagree

           1   2   3   4   5

      Comment:_____

      _____

      _____

      _____

      _____

      _____

      _____

      _____

      _____

      _____

      _____

19

(b)   "Religion is caught, not taught"

Strongly Agree	Agree	Unsure	Disagree	Strongly Disagree
1	2	3	4	5

(Please circle one number)

Comment:_____

_____

_____

_____

_____

_____

_____

_____

Finally, the questions which follow, although
personal, will only be used to "group" the answers in
an intelligible manner e.g., male teachers' answers
and female teachers' answers. BE ASSURED THAT THE
COMMENTS OF INDIVIDUAL TEACHERS OR SCHOOLS WILL NEVER
BE IDENTIFIED TO ANYONE.

33.   Please indicate your gender. (Please circle
appropriate number)

Male........1   Female......2

34.   What age are you now?   _____ years

35.   Is the school in which you teach mainly: (Please
circle one number)

Rural................................1

Small Town (under 10,000 people)......2

Large Town (10,000-100,000 people)....3

Suburban Area.........................4

City..................................5

20

36.   What type of school do you teach in? (Please circle one number)

REPUBLIC ONLY   NORTHERN IRELAND ONLY
Secondary School.........1   Grammar School......1

Community/Comprehensive..2   Secondary School....2

VEC (Community College)..3

VEC (Vocational School)..4

37.   How many students in your average R.E. Class? _____

38.   Please indicate your status by circling appropriate number:

                    Lay..............1

                    Priest...........2

                    Brother..........3

                    Sister...........4

THANK YOU FOR YOUR CO-OPERATION IN COMPLETING THIS QUESTIONNAIRE.

PLEASE RETURN THE COMPLETED QUESTIONNAIRE IN THE ENCLOSED PRE-PAID ENVELOPE TO:

                    John A. Weafer.
                    Director,
                    Council for Research and Development,
                    St. Patrick's College,
                    Maynooth,
                    Co. Kildare.

Introduction

Dermot A. Lane

Over the years, there have been rumours about the state of Religious Education in post-primary schools. It was often stated that very little doctrine was being taught and that many pupils left school with no real understanding of the Christian faith. Some even said that Religion had become something of 'a doss class', a place where anything and everything could be discussed without any educational direction or catechetical purpose. Sometimes these 'impressions' were accompanied by nostalgic pleas for a return to the surety of Sheehan's *Apologetics* and the clarity of *The Penny Catechism*.

The existence of this new Religious Education Teacher's Survey provides a context with hard data for an informed debate and discussion about the state of R. E. in post-primary schools. This survey will also help to shape future planning and policy making regarding R. E. in secondary schools and hopefully within the wider Christian community. The publication of the results of this Survey should initiate a new conversation about catechesis in schools and the community which, if heeded, could yield far-reaching positive educational and ecclesial re sults.

The Survey is scientific and was conducted with scrupulous care by the Council for Research and Development in Maynooth University under the able direction of John A. Weafer. Some educationalists might argue that cold statistics are not an adequate basis for evaluating the complexities of teaching, but it should be noted that the Survey also contains valuable and instructive autobiographical data.

Recent teacher surveys in England (1989) and Ireland (1991) have revealed a low level of morale among teachers. The causes are complex: stress, a lack of consultation and communication, discipline issues... We seem to be living at a time when teachers are not adequately valued by the community. This under-valuation of teachers also applies unfortunately to Religious Educators. And yet teachers are a nation's best asset, because they are the guardians of tradition, the inspirers of innovation, and the bearers of values. This R. E. Teachers' Survey, along with other Surveys, cries out for the provision of more in-service training and for new support systems. Teachers deserve the best they can be offered from the community. If this Survey, along with the others, stirs the consciences of those in a position to improve the situation, then it will have been a worthwhile exercise.

In reading the results, it should be borne in mind that this Survey is the first of its kind and it gives voice for the first time to a much taken-for granted, extremely hardworking, dedicated group of people variously described as Religion Teachers, Catechists and Religious Educators. School catechists are the unsung heroes and heroines of the Christian community, who day in and day out promote and defend, express and image, communicate and celebrate the riches of the Christian faith - at times against all kinds of odds. Teaching Religion is not easy, especially in times of great social and cultural upheaval. The cultural carriers of faith to-day no longer enjoy the stability of former generations and this makes it difficult to communicate the meaning of faith. The commitment, constructive criticism and enthusiasm of Religious Educators evident in this Survey is something that should be welcomed and valued by all.

To be sure, the work of Religious Educators in post-primary schools could be better. That is clearly evident in the Survey. Indeed, one of the purposes of the Survey is to effect improvements in the future. At the same time, it would be ungenerous to fail to recognise the outstanding contribution Catechists have made over the years in the education of young people in the Christian faith. This contribution has included the task of enabling students to cope with the changes of the Second Vatican Council and the cultural shifts that have occurred in Ireland since then.

One of the many striking features about the Survey is the finding that a majority of Religion Teachers are lay people and that over the last twenty years, a new body of catechetically qualified lay people have been quietly working away in bringing the Good News to young people in post-primary schools. A form of lay ministry, the presence of co-responsibility and collaboration within the Christian community, is already a part of ecclesial life in Ireland. The next chapter in the story of R. E. in Ireland must surely include the extension of this development into adult community education.

Another significant feature of the Survey is the presence of an 'internal dialogue' among the Catechists within the Survey itself. This 'internal dialogue' can be seen in relation to complex questions like the aims of Religious Education, the possibility of public examinations in Religion, the meaning of the statement 'Religion is caught and not taught', and the role of other agencies in catechesis. It is important that this 'internal dialogue' among the practitioners in the field be recognised in future discussions.

Given the significance of the Survey, it was decided that its publication should be accompanied with short commentaries by a sample of people closely associated with the work of R. E. : a catechist, a principal, a Diocesan Advisor, a teacher, a view from the North of Ireland, a parent and a bishop. Each was invited to give an initial reaction from their particular perspective.

The publication of this survey happily coincides with the commencement of a national debate on education in the context of a proposed new Education Act. A public debate on education must surely include reference to the importance of Religious Education. It is hardly fanciful to surmise that this Survey will have something to contribute to the wider debate. Let us hope that the emerging dialogues about education and Religious Education will be conducted in a spirit of openness, respect and trust.

Comment from a catechist

Ann Looney

The subjects of Religion, Religion teaching and Religion classes invariably engender strong feelings and opinions. Increasingly Religion is being spoken of as something to grow out of rather than into, as a source of oppression rather than freedom and as the last bastion of conservatism in an otherwise truly liberal world. Religion classes? Memories of these have entertained many a dinner party and lounge-bar gathering. The story of the nun and the Telephone Directory or the one about the Bishop and the Confirmation Questions, have been told and retold with many embellishments and adaptations. And Religion is always taught by nuns and priests or by a Christian Brother the latter having a high level of credibility and esteem given his role as U. 16 hurling coach! Lay teachers don't really feature in the general perception of Religion teaching. The classical lay Religion teacher is Frank O' Connor's infamous Mrs Ryan who was responsible for the sacramental preparation of Jackie and his friends in the short story 'First Confession'. She was eccentric, to put it mildly, dressed like a large vampire bat and told stories of sinners burning in hell and leaving marks on people's furniture. Thankfully she is a long way from the Religion teachers who took part is this most welcome survey!

The only thing shared by Mrs Ryan and the majority of R. E. teachers today is their lay status. 70.9% of Religious Education teachers are lay people, the majority of whom choose to do this work out of a personal interest in teaching Religion. This will come as a surprise to many people, perhaps even to R. E. teachers themselves who still face the 'you're a what?' response from incredulous inquirers. This high proportion of young, lay, qualified Religious Education teachers – the younger the teacher the more likely he or she is to have formal qualifications – who have chosen RE teaching as a career will raise more than a few of the 'Religion is disappearing' brigade. Such a large number of professionally qualified lay teachers of Religion poses several new challenges.

The first of these challenges is to the profession itself. Religion and the teaching of Religion are more than just subjects of nostalgic anecdotes. They are contentious issues, particularly at this time when the second level education system is being restructured and there is more discussion of the implications of the Green Paper and the forthcoming Education Act. The Bishops have already had words with the Minister on the question of the ethos of schools under Catholic trusteeship. So too have school managers. But on this issue, as with the Aids education debate, as with as many issues in the past, R.E. teachers have been silent. It seems bizarre that at a time when the gradual and not so gradual disappearance of youth from churches, and the growth of urban disaffiliation from formal Religion is sending shock waves through the hierarchy – no one has heard from the Religion teachers! Why is this so? One reason – without meaning to sound like a perspective candidate for the Presidency – is that as a group the teachers of Religious Education at second level have no voice. While the Catechetical Association of Ireland makes heroic efforts in this regard it draws its members from the primary and adult education sectors as well and has too few members at second level to be in any way representative. Therefore, the challenge to the profession is to find a voice, to make itself heard. But to whom must it speak?

It must speak to the Church. The second challenge which arises out of such a large number of lay people working in Religious Education is a challenge to the whole Church. Religious Education is an ecclesial activity. It is part of the evangelizing mission of the Church and, as people who work in the service of that mission, Religious Educators should be seen as ministers. Because the Religious Education of the young is carried out in the formal school setting, the ecclesial dimension is often neglected. While the primacy of the parents as the educators of their children in all the dimensions of life – including the religious – is recognised, in practice Religious Education is 'done' in schools. Therefore Religious Educators experience the difficulties of a dual role – minister of the Church and agent of the educational institution.

One of the reports most interesting sections deals with the quality to the relationship between school based Religious Education and the local parish community. Almost 90% of those who responded to the survey saw the need for greater co-operation between the school and the parish. But of those who had worked in co-operation with parishes in the past, a disturbingly high proportion – almost 47% – had mixed feelings about, were not satisfied or were totally dissatisfied with the experience (Chap. 5, Table 5. 9). And almost 20% found the chaplain to be 'unco-operative' or 'uninterested' (Chap. 4, Table 4. 14). When teachers met parishioners on an individual basis - the parents of the students – a much higher level of satisfaction was expressed. Parents were seen to be 'interested', 'encouraging' and 'supportive' of the work of Religious Education in the school. It would seem therefore, that there is plenty of goodwill from parents and teachers for greater parish-school links. But goodwill is not enough. Some structures are needed and generally, when any formal links with the parish are made the initiative comes from the school. Perhaps it is time for local parish communities and their leaders – clergy and lay people – to begin to own Religious Education as a task for the whole community, and the Religious Educator as a minister to that community. Now words like 'minister' and 'community' can set alarm bells ringing in the ear of many a Religious Educator. Words like this invariably lead to words like 'after school hours' and 'week-ends' and 'voluntary'. Many of these words are part and parcel of the RE teachers life, but does the recognition by the local community of its role in the Religious Education of the young mean that such things become standard practice and standard expectation? Is this what the acknowledgement of the ministerial dimension of the work of the Religious Educator means? Or does it mean that as ministers, Religious Educators are supported in their work by the parish community and by the Church as a whole?

Such support, it would seem, is sadly lacking. The survey shows that the educational community of the school, while the administration was generally perceived as giving a high profile to Religious Educators only 41% of respondents felt that it had a high profile among the staff. While some comments indicated that the staff were helpful and supportive, more said that they just were not interested (Chat. 4, Table 4.1). Now while R.E. teachers could easily be accused of disinterest in the work of Science or Irish teachers, statistics like these make interesting reading for those currently reflecting on the nature of the Catholic school The staff room then is not where support for the work of the Religious Educator is found. The parish and its lack of support has already been discussed. What then of the church as a whole? What does it offer in the way of support for these ministers of Religious Education?

One way in which it does support the work of Religious Educators in school is in the provision of text books for use in the classroom. One section of the report is devoted to these and to an evaluation of their usefulness. Most were found to be quite helpful, and suggestions were made as to how to improve these. An interesting fact which emerges is that a much lower level of satisfaction was expressed with senior texts than with junior ones (Chap. 3, Table 3.3). It is also worth noting that the survey was carried out prior to the publication of the Gill and Macmillan series for junior cycle.

Another way in which the Church supports the work of Religious Educators is in the provision of inservice training. 53% of respondents said they had attended at least one such course in the last five years (Chap. 1, Table 1.8). Because this training is provided by the Church rather than by the Department of Education, it must be paid for by the teacher and taken in the teacher's own time. This is yet another sign of the high level of commitment of those involved in R.E.. The survey didn't ask who had organised these courses. Most are usually offered by Training Colleges or by Religious Institutes around the country. I wonder how many of these were offered by a diocese to its teachers? Which brings us to the subject of diocesan adavisors.

While satisfaction was expressed with the helpfulness of the diocesan advisors, when asked to elaborate on their replies a large number of respondents expressed negative comments. 179 said they had little or no contact, and 144 said that she or he was unhelpful. But with no national catechetical office to support them and a huge number of schools to to work with, diocesan advisors can do little except make the occasional visit. It is interesting to note that the highest level of dissatisfaction was expressed by the teachers working in Dublin where there is the highest concentration of schools. If the church is to begin to recognise the work of Religious Educators as the work of the Church, as part of the mission of that Church then those in authority must begin to support them in that work.

As well as shedding light on the relationship between the Religious Educator and the wider community, this survey also provides insight into what happens within the classroom. The second chapter on the respondents experience of teaching Religious Education should be studied by all who are concerned by the fall-off in religious practices among the young, and among the not so young. Such cultural changes – as with the changes in familial patterns – will have immediate impact in the Religion classroom. Therefore it is inevitable that the great religious 'switch off' will manifest itself in R.E. class.

The survey noted that while the majority of teachers found the experience of teaching Religion 'rewarding' a large number said that 'pupils are not interested' (Section 2.2). It is worthwhile pointing out that of the 50.6% of respondents who wanted to see RE as a Leaving Certificate subject the highest proportion wanted it to increase pupil motivation and to give the subject more status (Section 5, Table 5.5). Only 32.8% wanted an examination at Junior Certificate level. In fact the pupi! responses to what happens in the classroom seemed to be the most important factor in determining the success or failure of Religious Education. When asked what impact the teachers would want Religious Education to have on the life of the student the majority aimed 'to encourage responsibility and personal development' (Section 5.2). Only 10 people said the aim should be to 'pass on the faith'. Pupil responses also supplied 'criteria of worthwhileness'. If a class was perceived as worthwhile for the pupils it was because they saw it as 'interesting and relevant'. As it noted in a comment on table 2.14, 'most Religious Education teachers consider a class to be worthwhile when it is of benefit to pupils rather than themselves. As table 2.15 shows, a class was worthwhile for the teachers if the pupils were interested. 'Giving the necessary information' featured well down the list of factors contributing to a worthwhile class.

What comes across from the data is the pupil centredness of the Religious Education classroom. If the pupils own lives and experiences are being taken seriously then it is clear which topics will be the most difficult to deal with. Table 2.17 shows that sexuality and sacraments top of the list of difficult subjects and it is at senior level that most difficulty is found. What seems surprising is that a higher proportion of young and formally trained teachers found difficulty with these subjects than teachers without qualifications. Surely the enthusiastic young qualified teacher should have no problem dealing with these subjects. Or could it be that such a teacher is more acutely aware of the fact that pupils life experiences challenge traditional teaching on these subjects? And that such a teacher, committed to the pupils' own experiences and Church teaching, finds it difficult to establish any dialogue between these two? Could it be so?

In Groomian terms, has the dialectical hermeneutic become diametrical? In fact Groome himself averted to this phenomenon on a recent visit to Ireland. Speaking at the Mount Oliver Institute he spoke of the new perception of the Religious Educator as theologian, enabling people of all ages to do their own theology. Referring to David Tracy's description of good theology as honouring the criteria of adequacy to experience and the criteria of appropriateness to the tradition, Groome said that these could also apply to the work of the Religious Educator. There was discussion among those working with Tom Groome on the course as to whether there is now a possibility that being adequate to experience might lead to inappropriateness to the tradition. This would make the dialectical hermeneutic stage of shared Christian Praxis difficult, if not impossible. This is a question of great relevance for Religious Educators most of whom, whether consciously or unconsciously, work out of some form of shared Christian Praxis.

Teachers in urban areas will be fascinated by table 4.2 and the insights it gives into whether teachers believe Religion has a high profile among students, in particular among senior students. Various surveys in recent years have told us that religious practice, sacramental attendance and Church affiliation are on the decline in Ireland. Statistically urban areas are well below rural in this regard. But some of the figures on table 4.2 seem to belie the national trend. 26% of teachers in rural areas believe that RE has a high profile among senior students compared with 40% of those in the city areas. In Dublin 32% of teachers see it as having a high profile among students but in Munster it is only 22.5%. The fact that Dublin has the highest proportion of formally trained Religion teachers could by a factor in this peculiar statistical turn around. But there must be other reasons. Could it be that in urban areas teachers have had to take account of the fact that growing numbers of those in the classroom are non-practising? Therefore, these teachers have had to re-shape their Religious Education accordingly. Could it be that the difficulty of making the course relevant has been solved by re-making the course. As well as a la carte Catholics, do we now have a la carte Religious Educators. In a recent article in *The Furrow*, Michael Paul Gallagher noted that people only turn to the *à la carte* menu when the *table d'hôte* is too bland, or doesn't offer wide enough variety to suit the appetites of the various diners. Have the Religious Educators begun to switch menus in an effort to satisfy the spiritual hunger of the students?

This survey would have failed if it had answered all the questions without generating new ones. And it has generated some exciting questions, questions that challenge the whole Christian community. But the greatest challenge is to Religious Educators themselves. The silence of Religious Educators – a silence of the lambs perhaps – has been ended by this survey. The first words have been spoken in what will prove to be a most important dialogue for the Irish Church.

The perspective of a principal

Elizabeth Cotter

The publication of *Whither Religious Education? A Survey of Post-primary Teachers in Ireland* provides a welcome opportunity to contribute to the on-going debate promised by the minister for Education, Mary O'Rourke, in preparation for the forthcoming Education Act. I welcome the debate in that it provides all those involved in education with the opportunity to reflect upon and assess the importance of education in the lives of our students and indeed for the future well-being of society. What is the role of the Catholic School? How to foster and develop its special characteristics? What is the place of Religious Education in the curriculum? How to provide on-going support for those involved in Religious Education in an increasingly individualistic, examination orientated, competitive and secularist education system? These are some of the questions that the publication of the Weafer-Hanley survey brings to our attention. It is the responsibility and privilege of Management to respond.

Recent Church documents highlight the importance of the Catholic School as an agent of evangelisation. The School provides a unique opportunity for collaboration with those other partners on the evangelising process, viz the family and the Parish. However, unless the School takes the initiative in encouraging and developing home-school and school-parish links, it is unlikely that this will happen elsewhere. Hence the recent growth in ministries e.g. Home-School liaison, lay Chaplaincy and Parish ministries of many kinds. The entire School Community provides the environment and context in which faith grows and develops. The R. E. teachers, with their skill and expertise, however, play a unique and invaluable role. We must therefore pay particular attention to the strengths and difficulties brought to our attention by this survey. We must ensure that the strengths are built upon and developed and that the difficulties are faced and dealt with. For the shape of Religious Education in the future depends in no small measure on the Catechists and Catechetical Teams in our schools.

R. E. Teachers are aware that there are other effective means of getting across the Christian message (5.3). With Junior pupils, the home-school link provides a more effective means of evangelisation. For Senior students however, the parish situation is more effective (5.5). The onus is on management, therefore, to foster and support initiatives which aim to develop collaboration with Family and Parish. Since faith is handed on and developed within the context of the entire faith community, the family and parish must be encouraged to play their part. The school, because of its contacts with parents and the wider community, is in a unique position to encourage this development. Since students are in school during one of the most critical and formative periods of their development, the part in the evangelisation process played by the school is a vital and necessary one. It is in the school that the young person acquires much knowledge of his/her faith and learns the skills necessary to help on the life-long journey of faith. But it is the family and Parish which provides the support and nurturance necessary for the greater part of this journey. R. E. teachers rightly indicate that greater cooperation among the partners in the evangelisation process is the way forward. (5.8.)

It is encouraging to note the positive response from those teaching R.E. The experience is rewarding and challenging for the majority (2.1). Personal interest in the task which they perceive to be very important, keeps many in the teaching profession (2.3). A significant number believe their experience of teaching R. E. has changed for the better in recent years (2.7). There is positive feedback on the support given by Principals (4.1), Chaplains (4.5), family (4.14) and Parishes where cooperation with schools exists (5.8). General satisfaction was expressed with the time given to R. E. classes (4.6) and with resources available to R. E. personnel (3.8). Texts remain the most popular resource despite difficulties of language, content and presentation in some. (3.3). The diversity of texts used at Senior level reflects the teachers' need to provide greater stimuli at this level and to find ways to motivate students of this age-group.

However, it is a cause for concern that a substantial number perceived the teaching of R. E. as difficult (2.1). Almost one in ten usually found it a very difficult experience (2.1). One in ten cite their Principal's orders as the major reason for continuing to teach R. E. (2.4). Less than half of those surveyed believe that R.E. had a high profile with other staff members (4.2). Only 30% felt R.E. had a high profile among senior pupils.

These statistics must be taken seriously if School authorities are to ensure the future well-being of Religious Education in our schools. Nevertheless, it is important to remember that teachers in general are experiencing difficulty at the present time. Many teachers suffer from high levels of stress. The changing sociological patterns in Ireland and the increased expectations and demands made on schools, contribute in no small measure to this situation. Curricular innovations have changed the nature of teaching itself.

Catechists, however, are not strangers to the new approaches. Indeed, in many schools, Catechetical teams have spear-headed the multi-disciplined approach to teaching. For those untrained in new approaches however, the demands of teaching today can be particularly trying.

Particular difficulties were expressed by those teaching Senior cycle R.E. (2.19). Many teachers believe that the introduction of R.E. as an examination subject would provide the motivation necessary for students at this level (5.3). R.E. teachers believe that care must be taken, however, to retain the faith dimension. Principals and Boards of Management must enter into this dialogue so that the merits and disadvantages associated with making R.E. an examination subject, can be thoroughly analysed and agreed upon. For it is only by working together on this issue that Management and R.E. personnel will be able to give sufficient weight to make the proposal a viable proposition with the Education Authorities.

Management has huge responsibility to ensure that maximum advantage is taken of the school situation. Resources must be given to those involved in the work of Religious Education. In these days of ever more stringent budgetary constrictions on the part of Principals and School Authorities, it is imperative that the work of Religious Education is and is seen to be given top priority in terms of personnel, finance and resources. This can be done e.g. by giving priority to the requests of R.E. personnel when time - tabling; by providing material resources, finance and facilities; by ensuring that there is time for formal and informal meetings; by attendance at these meetings; by evaluation of R.E. programmes with R.E. personnel at the end of each year; by monitoring the impact of R.E. on the life of the School Community; by keeping R.E. on the agenda of Staff Meetings despite the demands of maintenance problems, finance, discipline and the multiplicity of other tasks that are the daily concern of the busy Principal; by providing personal and professional In-service on a regular basis; by developing a team approach to share the challenges and the concerns of Religious Educators. The attitude, value system and behaviour of the Principal, demonstrates most clearly the importance of R.E. in the life of the school community. Principals and Managers, therefore, must be aware of their power and consciously use it to promote the welfare of R.E. in our schools.

As we prepare for the introduction of an Education Act, the future is in our hands. Decisions made now will influence future generations. Do we believe sufficiently in the value of our Catholic School system to ensure it takes its rightful place in the pluralist Ireland of the future? Are we willing, despite the demands on our time, resources and personnel, to provide what ever is necessary to promote the well-being of Religious Educators in our schools? Are we ready to give priority to the work of Religious Education within the overall curriculum?

We are at a crossroads in the history of Irish education. We have the power and the resources necessary at this point in time, to influence the shape of the future. Our most important resource lies in the quality and commitment of the teachers in our schools. The Weafer-Hanley survey clearly points this out. Our R.E. teachers believe in the importance of what they are doing ; they have indicated their willingness to collaborate with administrators, other staff members, family, parish, youth groups and so on. It is the task of Management to harness this tremendous potential in the service of the Kingdom. Principals and Management Boards must provide the leadership and the conditions necessary to carry out this task efficiently and effectively. I believe that collaboration is the key to progress. The degree to which we are willing to work together, constantly challenging, stimulating and supporting one another, will determine the fruitfulness of our labours.

The Weafer-Hanley survey, in highlighting the strengths and difficulties of those involved in Religious Education in our Schools, has provided an invaluable insight into the present situation. It has given to Principals and Managers, clear indications of the needs and difficulties of R.E. teachers. Principals must listen to what has been said and respond appropriately. This challenge must be taken up: Principals and Managers, the future of Religious Education in Ireland is in your hands.

Response from a Diocesan Advisor

Cóirle McCarthy

I am grateful for the opportunity to comment briefly on this important survey. I am reviewing it from my perspective both as a Catechist and a Diocesan Advisor. I have felt for a long time that there was a need for such a document and so am pleased that such a comprehensive, relevant and scientific survey of what is happening in Religious Education is available to us. My initial reaction is one of hope, enthusiasm and a great sense that there is a future for Religious Education within our second level educational system with far reaching possibilities. This is in contrast to my own perception of Religious Education, where I see the thrust for the future as being more home/parish based, and yet a high level of satisfaction is expressed in the survey for school based Religious Education. Though Table 5.3 and Table 5.5 recognise that there are other ways of getting across the Christian message, I was quite surprised also to note the findings of Table 5.9 which reflected the level of satisfaction with parish co-operation. This would not be altogether my experience as I move around among Religious Educators.

Of the number of teachers surveyed, 54% of the respondents had formal qualifications, while 46% did not (Section 1.4.4). This is a very genuine reflection of the situation as I experience it, and it is borne out further on in the report when it states in 1.4.4 that 'a higher proportion of teachers in the Dublin area had formal catechetical qualifications than in other regions'. The reality is that 'formal qualifications, as outlined in Table 1.5 are only available in the Leinster region and this precludes access for many who may wish to pursue this choice of career. This has been a real difficulty to those of us involved in Religious Education, because, when appointments are being made in schools, the pool of qualified candidates is very small. Maybe the situation might be addressed as a result of this survey. It is a priority as I understand it.

I was at the same time surprised and encouraged by many of the findings of the survey. One example of this is that so many teachers found the experience of teaching Religion challenging and rewarding (Table 2.1). Despite the fact that many teachers work against such odds as apathy, lack of interest etc., that there are possibilities for greater things to happen must give us all reason for continuing to believe and hope in our common task.

Another reason for optimism in the survey is that the majority of teachers continue to teach Religious Education because of personal interest in the subject (Table 2.4), as well as the findings of Table 5.6 where it reveals that 'a teacher's own faith is a vital component in fostering faith in the classroom'. These findings challenge us to continue to nourish, support and provide opportunities for faith development/renewal for our teachers of Religious Education. It is also heartening to note the results of Table 1.8 which indicates the number who attended in-service courses, most of which were classroom oriented.

Table 5.10, and further analysis of it, indicates 'a variety of in-service experiences which would be of assistance to them in teaching Religious Education'. As we try to implement and act on the findings of this survey, some of these needs must be met. It must be said that many dioceses offer such courses/seminars for their teachers, but it is done with little or no recognition from the Department of Education and one is always relying on the the good-will and co-operation of school administration.

This leads me to look at the issue of support for Religious Education in our schools. As I have said, for the most part, we rely on the generosity and interest of school administrators, and I want to acknowledge the level of support for Religious Education by school principals. Table 4.1 of the survey reflects this. However in some instances it is my experience that the level of support is there only in theory and not in practice. An example of this is the failure to appoint a catechist in a school when an opportunity arises and some other examination subject gets priority. Various reasons are given for this but one wonders what is the real status of Religious Education in our schools. Further it is interesting to note from Table 4.1 and 4.2 that the level of support for, and status of Religious Education in school administration is not reflected among the staff and senior pupils, while it is a priority for junior pupils. There are of course many and varied reasons why the situation pertains, some of which are given in the survey. An example of this can be seen in Section 4.2 of the survey, where 118 respondents claimed that Religious Education was 'perceived as important' by school staff: an almost equal number of respondents (113) claimed 'that staff were not interested in Religious Education'. Section 4.2 indicates that senior students for the most part are not interested in Religious Education.

All of this is saying something very serious to us. It certainly is the situation in our schools. The challenge is to recognise that a problem does exist, particularly in Religious Education at senior level. Reaction to *The Living Faith Series*, as I experienced it, has not been positive. Yet teachers use it in the absence of something more helpful. On the other hand, I suggest that the problem is greater than any number of texts will answer. Religious Education must happen in our schools, but, on the basis of this evaluation, another more effective way must be found. In some instances, with great co-operation, compromise and careful planning, alternative ways are being used. For example, small groups of approximately 15 pupils per teacher in a team teaching arrangement has proved quite successful. It certainly allows for greater participation, a more personal approach and a higher level of interest. It provides opportunities for greater informality in approach and this makes the subject real and more accessible. Obviously to use such an approach will require greater resources, personnel and otherwise as Table 4.3 clearly suggests.

To comment briefly on the resource question, the whole survey indicates the need for more formally trained teachers of Religious Education. Each school ought to have, at least, one Religious Education teacher with recognised formal training, who would act as a resource person to the other teachers of Religious Education in the school, and who would co-ordinate other resources required. The challenge to do this must be placed before our schools. Very few subjects are taught by people who have no professional competence. This I believe would go a long way towards answering the need for more resources. It would enable changes to occur in Religious Education programmes, and would improve the status of Religious Education in our schools.

The survey noted that while most teachers talked to individual parents (Table 4.12), the qualifications of the teachers were found to be significant. 'Teachers with no qualifications were less likely(48.5%) than those with formal (80%) or semi-formal (72%) Religious Education qualifications to talk to parents'. The percentage of teachers from Dublin/Leinster region who talked with parents was greater than in other areas, and this is further linked with findings of Table 4.12.

The report examined the question of Religion as an examination subject. I was disappointed that examination was the only area of accountability mentioned in the report. I suggest that the need for accountability in Religious Education is a very real one. If it is to be credible at all, it must take its place equally among all other disciplines. I further suggest that it needs to be an integral part of Religious Education for the future. However, in Table 5.3 of the survey, the majority of teachers favoured Religious Education as an examination subject in the Leaving Certificate, but a significant minority disagreed for a multiplicity of reasons. The conclusion I came to from this, and from my own experience, depends on which model of Religious Education one operates out of. Religious Education as an examination subject is not the answer. Other means and methods of assessment/accountability must be researched and tried. The revised *Christian Way 1*, 'Love One Another', has an in-built method of assessment of what pupils have learned, and this is at least one step in that direction.

This brings me to the question of text books. My experience fits well with the findings of the survey where the use of texts is concerned. The *Christian Way* series is the most widely used in most of the schools I visit. Religious Education at junior level appears to be reasonably healthy and most of the suggestions for improvement made in the survey, with regard to language and concepts, presentation, content and relevance have been taken on board in the revised version *Christian Way 1* 'Love One Another', Maura Hyland, (Veritas '90/91). This text book was carefully researched and hopefully will meet the needs of teachers of junior cycle Religious Education. It is envisaged that a similar pattern will follow in *Christian Way II* and *III*, where indeed greater problems are experienced. Where the text book or some specific course is not followed, I sometimes wonder is the syllabus for Religious Education adhered to or just any haphazard programme followed? These are important issues for those of us who take Religious Education seriously. We need to constantly assess what we are doing as Religious Educators, and how we are, in fact, doing it.

In the survey Tables 3.2 and 4.3.3 indicated the findings with regard to the use of text books at senior level, which showed that the great majority of teachers used the *Living Faith* series. However, I would like to have seen a further, more in-depth, analysis of how teachers actually perceived this series. My own perception is that while most teachers at senior level use the text initially, it is eventually discarded for a variety of reasons. I referred the this earlier in my review. While I say this, I recognise that no one text book will adequately cater for senior cycle students.

As I said at the outset, the survey is both encouraging and challenging. However I wonder is it a little optimistic? It does demand a very positive and real response. It challenges the commonly held perception that Religious Education is a dying cause! It provides us with a very sound basis for future planning in Religious Education. My hope is that it will be a source of information and inspiration for all of us who are involved in and interested in handing on the Christian message.

COMMENTARIES

The views of a teacher

Brian Mooney

As a teacher of other subjects and Religious Education, I have been asked to write a short commentary on the findings of the Religious Education Teachers' Survey. Most of the data relating to the status of Religious Education in our schools, the level of motivation of our students and teachers and the depth of knowledge acquired by the student accurately reflects, in my experience, the reality of R. E. in our schools.

It is often argued that statistical information can be interpreted to suit any individual point of view. I hope I have not fallen into that trap and that my comments are in tune with the overall findings of the Survey. There were many areas of interest on which I could have written but I decided to narrow my focus for the purpose of this short commentary to the relationship between R.E. and the school environment.

All the research findings point to the fact that within the present school environment the status of R.E. is handicapped by uncertainty as to the goals to be achieved. I would argue that acquisitions of Religious knowledge is the primary responsibility of the R.E. class. The Faith Development of the student is the overall responsibility of (a) the home, (b) the entire teaching staff, including the R.E. teachers and the chaplain, and (c) the parish. A solid base in Religious knowledge enhances the student's faith development and this will only be acquired if R.E. is given the same standing as all other bodies of knowledge in the education system, i.e., assessment through the formal State examination system. We are fortunate that this recommendation can be supported by the very positive findings in the Survey from the Northern Ireland schools where this already occurs.

The acquisition of Religious knowledge is a major educational undertaking which requires the use of the following skills: learning, concentration, study, written work, reflection, discussion, etc. Young people are very familiar with this process. It takes place in class and at home and is a normal part of their daily life and the success or failure of their efforts is judged by their performance in their terminal examination. This is their world and, as an experienced teacher, it is perfectly clear to me that students judge all activity in the classroom in relation to its relevance in passing their terminal examination.

I have noticed that students in first year treat R.E. class like any other subject, but by the end of first year they discover that it is not a State examination subject at either Junior or Leaving Certificate level and so they subsequently cease to treat it as a serious subject. This argument is supported by information supplied by Veritas Publications, who informed me that the sale of first year R.E. text books was on a par with all other subjects, that this figure declined in second and third year and fell sharply in Senior Cycle. This simple confirms for me what I already believed, that once students become aware they are not going to be formally examined in R. E., they cease to see it as 'a real subject'. This view is also supported by the comments in Section 4.3 of the report:

- 'More interested in exams' (128)
- 'Indifference/disinterested' (99)
- 'Doss class' (54)
- 'Irrelevant to their lives' (28)
- 'Only important because of R.E. exams' (21)

Not only do the students cease to see it as a 'real' subject, so do the majority of the teaching staff (section 4.2). 42% of teachers/staff see R.E. as having a high status.

In summation, the factors mentioned above:

(a) The Northern Ireland experience;
(b) Text book sales;
(c) Student attitude to subject;
(d) Staff attitude to subject

demonstrate clearly that the non-examination nature of the subject seriously hampers the achievement of the goals set for the subject.

Some would argue that to make R.E. an examination subject would destroy the Faith Development nature of the subject. I believe the opposite to be the case. Religious faith is developed through the interactive process between the young Christian and all other members of the community from the moment of birth. Within the school context, this means all interactions between staff and students, and among the students themselves. What a deeply enriching and challenging vision it is for all involved in education to realise that the faith development of our students is directly dependent on the nature of all our relationships with them and not just that of the R.E. teachers. At present, we are not challenged with this vision because all things religious are considered to be the responsibility of the R.E. teacher in his/her R.E. class and this perspective robs the subject teacher of this challenging vision.

Not only does the present system rob the other subject teachers of a role in faith development, it also tends to rob the chaplain of one. I have sympathy for chaplains who find great confusion arising regarding their roles in schools. Many principals are unsure of what the chaplain should be doing and this often leads to misunderstandings. Many R.E. teachers also feel that chaplains should be doing more to help them, but they are also unsure of what that 'something' should be. Chaplains are not teachers and asking them to take a class every now and again is not the answer. But, in our present system, with all religious matters being identified with the R.E. class, chaplaincy activity tends to be identified with this period. In an exam-based system, where the faith-life of the school would be seen as over and above the R.E. class, the chaplain's role becomes clearer because he/she becomes the central figure in guiding/directing the overall school community to enrich and deepen the quality of its faith life.

I suggest therefore that many students leave the education system with a very poor knowledge of the underlying principles of religious belief because acquiring them requires solid, hard work which is only undertaken in our system in examination subjects. We may lament this fact as being deplorable, but it is nevertheless a fact. Later, when confronted by the various crises of life, they find themselves bereft of a level of understanding of moral and religious matters that would enable them to deal with these crises. Therefore our second level educational system is failing in its primary role, i.e., preparing young people to become mature adult members of society and the Christian community. Our system in its present structure also denies the overall school community its proper role in faith formation.

Finally, I would strongly support formal examinations in Religious Education. I believe it would lead to R.E. as a subject being treated more seriously than at present. Students would acquire an understanding of Scripture, the underlying principles of Christian moral reasoning, the doctrinal basis of the Catholic faith and a deeper understanding of the meaning of the Sacraments. How they applied this knowledge in their own lives would depend to a large extent on the quality of lived faith they experienced during their school years and also later in life their home, parish and work environments. I believe the points I have made are fully supported by the data as outlined in the Religious Education Teachers' Survey and I hope they will be of some value in the ongoing debate in these matters.

A voice from the North of Ireland

Sean Cahill

Twenty years ago the Ecclesiastical Inspectors of Down & Connor Diocese asked the principal teacher of a secondary (intermediate) school in a small town about the state of Religion among his pupils. The pupils had one class of R.E. each day. All made a one day Retreat; confessions were 'general' at Christmas and Easter. Yet he was gravely pessimistic. 'Father' he said, 'I can tell you I worry about it. I wonder if we're having any effect on them at all. Their reverence for the Mass is going and they are even losing their respect for their elders.' He elaborated for the benefit of his visitors. 'Last Sunday I saw three of the senior pupils in the parish Church. They were standing on the stairs leading to the gallery during Mass. Do you know Father, when I told them to go into 'the seats' and attend Mass properly, they were very reluctant; very reluctant, Father. I could see by their looks that they resented me telling them to move. Now that wouldn't have happened in this town a few years ago, Father. I don't know if the religious programme is working properly.'

I recall our conversation as we drove away after our visit. The Dean in the Diocesan College would hardly dare to make such an approach to boarders at the Mass in College Chapel; and certainly principals in the post-primary schools in Belfast at that time would have been delighted to have had such a problem. In that particular year, one fourteen year old boy had been shot dead; two young girls from another city school died as bomb victims. He was worried about boys standing during Sunday Mass!

On the whole, we concluded that as long as we had concerned teachers of his calibre, Religious Education would remain sound in that town.

The incident came back to my memory when I reflected on *Whither Religious Education? A Survey of Post-primary Teachers in Ireland*. My initial reaction was that this puts on record what we already know from our Diocesan Advisors' visits. Our impression of principals, teachers, pupils, parents and chaplains in the post-primary schools were, and are, as the survey reported. The percentages were predictable. The findings, both negative and positive were what we would have expected.

However, more analytical reading would suggest that the overall findings of the survey would convince me that the principal of our small-town school (where he's still alive) would at least be convinced that all was not lost when his pupils sheepishly went from the gallery to the pew.

For the overall impression given by the survey is that his concerns, his worry, his implicit expression of the relationship of Religious Education to character, to decent values and to parish life, is strong in the post-primary schools of Ireland. It is very strong in the minds, hearts and convictions of our Religious Education teachers. The solace is in almost every area covered by this survey. A record for hope.

From the wealth of the remarks which were recorded to illustrate the flavour of the statistic I chose the following:

'If you are not committed yourself, there is no way you can find meaning or reward or in any way enhance the faith of the pupils.' 'To foster faith in the classroom, you must give enthusiasm and be enthusiastic. You must be willing to live as a Christian in the class; to forgive and be forgiven; to love even those you don't like in class; to keep starting again.'

'Relationship with students is essential - people generally acquire values of those whom they perceive as wholesome. Teachers and students must respect each other's dignity.'

'I feel Religion is both caught and taught. They will not follow our example unless we can teach them why all is important to us.'

'I love teaching (or trying to teach) Religion. I feel that even if the students don't respond as I would like now, I am giving them something important that will be with them for the rest of their lives.'

'The faith has to be caught, but a well structured class can ensure attitudes, values, information are learned, even if the teacher has little personal faith.'

'I believe that the moment a child asks 'why' about the wonder of life and receives an answer, this begins the teaching of Religion. You can catch Religion for a while, but it will wither without a solid background of knowledge and understanding to inspire that faith.'

'Most junior pupils see Religion as a subject like any other. They find it stimulating and enjoyable in general.'

What impression do they collectively make? To me, they speak of a generation of R.E. teachers who are witnesses to faith - professionals, catechists, prophets, in direct line with the headmaster two decades ago. I chose them because they were made by the younger teachers: all under thirty years. Not one of them was in a post-primary school when he was voicing his concern.

Another story from my earlier days as 'Ecclesiastical Inspector' may be appropriate here. A president of a boarding school rather petulantly remarked on the lack of appreciation of some parents. 'You know they should thank us that we help their boys to love their homes and families.' He went on to explain that the boarders idealised their homes, parents and family life during their experience of boarding school. The rebelliousness of their teenage years was exercised against the school, the teachers and, above all, those charged with boarders discipline and food.

Some of the most negative findings of the survey are about the pupil's attitudes to the religious classes and about their (the pupils') perception of the importance of Religious Education. Thus, even the young teacher's perception of 70% of senior pupils 'Religion is regarded as boring and irrelevant.' Perhaps that is true. Perhaps it is a perception! Yet somehow, like boarding school dinners, R.E. is still important and will sustain young people's faith.

Consider what the survey found among the R.E. teacher's:
(1) That in general teaching R.E. is a rewarding, if challenging experience – 59%.
(2) That personal interest in teaching, and in teaching R.E. in particular, was the motivation of 72% of R.E. teachers.
(3) That the experience of teaching R.E. has changed for the better during teachers' years in the classroom – 59%.
(4) That 87% use the R.E. text-books and find the teachers resources good or excellent – 60%.
(5) Administration in schools give R.E. a high profile – 69%.
(6) Principals are very helpful or, at least, helpful to R.E. teachers – 87% – as are chaplains 79%, and Diocesan Advisors 80%.
(7) R.E. teachers generally feel adequately or well prepared to teach Religion – 78%.

Coming from the North, I am expected to comment on the quality of replies from the 105 post-primary schools there, represented by 99 teachers of whom 42 were from my own diocese.

The North was over represented in the survey. It may have contributed to the positive outcome! The teachers there were even more positive about their experience in Religious Education.

They were practically all committed to public examination in Religious Education (93% did them) and were satisfied with the outcome (81% reported positively). This had its influence on the overall statistic which recorded a 51% option for public examination in R.E. Twice as many from the North felt that it would provide motivation in the classroom, especially among senior pupils, status for the subject and increased knowledge of the content of the programme. On the whole, that would help even if there was fear that examination in R.E. would destroy faith. I hope the 'souls' who thought so were not from the North, but have no means of telling!

The survey was not totally positive. Among the findings were statistics which might well cause alarm. For instance, 62.9% of the teachers had seriously considered giving up teaching R.E. However, during the very week I got my copy of this survey, a Teachers' Union in Northern Ireland published its findings of a survey conducted among its members. Over 80% of them had considered giving up teaching as a career! One city primary school was piloting an in-service course on 'coping with stress among teachers,' with a view to having it spread to all our schools!

I've referred to the 'agog with apathy' syndrome among senior pupils. There was evidence that R.E. teachers were not perceived as in the mainstream by their colleagues, nor was the subject highly esteemed by the parents. Parish links were wished for, but no great willingness to make them or to strengthen them was recorded.

Finally, there was the baffling returns about the Diocesan Avisors. Generally speaking, they were very helpful (27.5%) or helpful (53.6%).

Large numbers then went on to express negative comments in relation to the Advisors. By a majority of one, teachers recorded their impression of the Advisors as having little or no contact (179 teachers) rather than 'helpful and supportive' (178 teachers). A total of 185 said of their Advisors that they were 'good organisers' or 'helpful in some respects' and a further 65 commented positively on the Advisor's role in providing resources. Yet, there were 144 who described the Advisor as 'unhelpful.'

What is the explanation? No one who attends the Association of post-primary Advisors' gatherings will be shocked by these comments. For over a decade now one third of the Irish dioceses are unrepresented at such gatherings. Some dioceses who are represented have nominal Advisors for the post-primary schools. They are assigned to other duties as well as – full time curates in busy parishes, teachers in the diocesan schools, chaplains to the vocational college, etc.

The eleven teachers who wrote 'don't know what his/her role is' might well echo these Advisors' personal appraisal of themselves!

That area of the survey demands not just attention, but remedial action.

The provision of suitable pupil resources demands attention. Pre-service training and in-service provision are obvious needs for many of the R.E. teachers in Ireland.

The catechetical revolution began in the post-primary schools of Ireland just over twenty years ago with the introduction of *Christ with Us*. It departed from the dogmatic or knowledge-centred approach and centred on faith formation; linking the experience of the young to moral values and liturgical expression of faith. That the young trained teachers of today are so committed to their vocation justifies the effort and pain encountered during that revolution.

I have heard a catechist say that the school is unsuitable for the conduct of catechesis, because it is one of three places where the person is institutionalised without freedom. Prisoners are condemned to jail, the mentally ill are committed to the hospital and the young are sent to school.

There is one huge difference with the young however. All young people must go to school – just as all young people must go through teenage years to become mature.

Their pilgrimage through teenage years will be, for many of them, an enriching experience and a formative influence for good if the findings of this survey are used to build even more effective communities of Christian faith in the post-primary schools of our country. That solace I take from this survey. However, it shouldn't lead to complacency; indeed, the introduction expresses the hope that the findings will help all who are involved with faith formation of the young people to plan for the future with much more accurate estimates of the needs of school communities, of managers, of parents, parishes and above all, of teachers themselves and their pupils.

A word from a parent

Siobhan Riordan

As a parent I wholeheartedly welcome this survey and laud those who initiated it and those who carried out the research.

Not all topics dealt with within the scope of the survey will appear to have direct relevance to parents; nevertheless, anything that might better facilitate the spiritual development of our young people in post-primary schools must be seen to be of interest to parents in the long-term. Apart from the few topics which relate specifically to parents, therefore, I have selected a number of areas from the many subjects of a more general nature which, of necessity, constitute the bulk of the survey.

To supplement the statistical data, I shall include some comments made by individual respondents which were randomly chosen by the authors. Also, I consider it to be more practical to deal, in particular, with some of the negative aspects or problem areas relating to the subject matter and to put forward recommendations for their redress. The format will be as follows:
    (a) General subject-matter
    (b) Parent-related subject-matter
    (c) Recommendations

(a) General subject-matter

Preamble

The sample comprises 679 Religious Education teachers from Catholic post-primary schools both in the Republic of Ireland and in Northern Ireland. Of these 61% are lay and 39% religious personnel. (71% lay, 29% religious, are the corresponding figures in the 'National Profile' which appears in appendix A.) 52% of respondents have 'formal' qualifications e.i. they have pursued one of the following courses:
    A diploma/degree course at Mater Dei Institute
    A one-year course at Mount Oliver
    A qualification/degree in theology
    Teacher training qualification in Religious Education from Northern Ireland.
    A further 15% have completed a post-graduate diploma course, which, in the universities, is part-time, usually of two years duration.

Respondents' experiences of and attitudes to teaching Religious Education.

Parents will be reassured to find that teaching Religious Education is a rewarding, though challenging experience for the majority of respondents. It will cause them some concern, however, to discover that a substantial minority (38%) find it difficult and one in ten perceives it to be very difficult. What is even more disturbing is the fact that 37% have seriously thought of giving it up! When elaborating on their experiences, the respondents' two main observations were that 'Pupils are not interested' and that 'It is a challenge to reach youth.'

In teaching the subject, it would appear that those without 'formal'/ 'semi-formal' qualifications are more likely to experience difficulty than their qualified counterparts.

Also for many, difficulties are encountered when dealing with senior cycle pupils in particular. One respondent put it like this:

'At senior level, any topic that seems to be in any way with 'God' or 'formal Religious Instruction' turns pupils off completely, and this makes it impossible to teach them.'

Indeed, as regards 'topics', one of the more telling statistics in the survey must be that only 8% mention the Bible as having been the subject of a worthwhile class!

And although the majority of respondents find classes of 'mixed'/high ability' to be more worthwhile than those of 'low ability' – apparently there are difficulties right across the board. The following remark illustrates this:

'Often the weaker grades find the doctrine difficult to comprehend, while the brighter streams want logical and rational argument, and cannot comprehend 'mystery' or 'faith.'

Text books are considered useful in the teaching situation as regards presentation, assignments, real-life examples etc. But in relation to the students 'texts' in particular, there are criticisms of the difficult language and concepts used, the advanced and abstract nature of the content 'boring' and 'irrelevant' material etc. - all of which no doubt compound the other difficulties already outlined.

Respondents' attitudes to Religious Education as a public examination subject

Approximately 51% of respondents (with twice as many from the North than from the Republic) would favour the introduction of Religious Education as a Leaving Cert./GCSE subject. The largest number (N=25) feel that this would increase the motivation of pupils; a further

200 believe that it would increase the status of Religious Education, while 174 respondents hold that it would increase the pupils' knowledge. But 119 respondents are of the opinion that such a development would destroy the 'faith dimension' of Religious Education while, in a variety of responses, others cite the negative aspects of examinations *per se*.

Approximately 93% of N.I respondents already have Religious Education as a public examination subject in their schools. It is interesting to note, therefore, that given their experience in the matter, they appear to be more in favour of the 'examination' than their counterparts in the Republic – where Religious Education is not a public examination subject. And although, apparently, discussions on this matter have already taken place among some interested parties – it is to be hoped that parents will get an opportunity of playing a full part in any future debate and decision-making process on this potentially controversial issue.

Respondents' suggestions as to ways of assisting them in their teaching of Religious Education

Respondents gave their views on 'in-service' experiences and the other 'support services' which, they felt would assist them in their teaching of Religious Education. 'Training in methodology' and 'additional resources' were the choices of the largest proportion of the respondents. This finding ought to be viewed very seriously by all parties interested in the spiritual welfare of our youth. It constitutes an unequivocal recommendation by those directly involved as to how best they could be aided in the execution of their important and seemingly onerous task.

(b) Parent related subject matter

Matters relating specifically to parents are dealt with in Chapter 5 'Cooperation between school and parish', e.g. 73% of respondents talked to parents about the Religious Education of their children. Most of the discussions took place at parent-teacher meetings. The majority of respondents found these encounters helpful describing parents as 'interested' and 'supportive' and indicating how they, as teachers, learned more about their pupils e.g. background, problems etc. Approximately 13% found these interchanges to be unhelpful, citing as reasons 'parents' lack of interest in Religious Education', 'parents' greater interest in examinations' etc.

67% of respondents believed that pupils acquire faith through the 'witness' of others, i.e. that faith is 'caught' rather than 'taught'. 97 of respondents hold that this happens specifically in the home. But 168 respondents feel that faith is both 'caught' and 'taught'. One respondent put it this way:

'I do believe that a Godly/religious atmosphere in the home and neighbourhood is essential for fostering religious growth; but there is definitely a lot to be said for some knowledge to help one's own faith/conviction to grow.'

Another respondent's view is that 'faith is caught – Religion is taught.'

Not surprisingly therefore, the majority of respondents feel that further links ought to be forged between school, home and parish, one comment being that '... no group can do it alone in today's society'. Approximately half of those who did not wish for further cooperation between school and the wider community think that it is 'unrealistic', one opinion being that 'cooperation like that isn't possible when pupils come from such a wide variety of parishes.'

If one subscribes to the view that faith is 'caught', then a considerable responsibility regarding 'witness' rests with parents and the general community, including teachers. But it is also our duty to encourage all concerned to address any problems which might be in evidence specifically in the school situation in order to ensure the proper facilitation of the spiritual development of our children.

(c) Recommendations

(1) Two of the areas which are highlighted by respondents as regards helping them in their task are:
    (a) Training in methodology
    (b) More resources

(a) Training in Methodology

The organisers of Religious Education ought to give serious consideration to the regular provision of in-service courses encompassing a broad range of teaching methods in areas such as the following:
    (i) The presentation of Biblical themes
    (ii) Drama, mime, role-play, improvisation etc. to cater for the dimensions of 'mystery' and 'imagination' in Religious Education.
    (iii) All types of music that appeal to the spiritual side of the individual-Church, Classical, pop etc
    (iv) 'The media' in general but specifically the proper use of the video in Religious Education.
    (v) Techniques in the conduct of debates

Also, the organisers of post-graduate university diploma courses should be encouraged to give more time to methodology than is given at present.

(b) More resources

(i) A multi-resource centre

Consideration should be given to the establishment of a 'multi-resource centre' in each diocese in a suitably equipped building, centrally located. It should be manned by personnel who would be well versed in the availability, use, merits and demands of a variety of resources – a person/people who would have

(a) the specific talent relating to all resource materials.

(b) the time to share it with Religious Education teachers.

(ii) Parents as resources

Over 90% of respondents believe that there are methods other than the school of getting across the Christian message, vis. parents, parish, local community, church, priests, clubs, societies, social work etc. Parents therefore, could surely be used as 'resources' to supplement the school activity e.g. those involved in areas as lay ministry, social work, world issues, various voluntary organisations etc. could be brought periodically into the schools to talk on their particular subject or to facilitate group sessions. In this way the 'special interest' would be the determining factor regarding the choice of parents rather than the parish to which they belong. At the start of the school year, for example, a meeting could be organised in the school dealing with a broad 'pastoral care' dimension. Religious Education teachers, health education teachers, pastoral care teachers etc. could meet with parents to establish specific 'caring links' and to identify areas of relevant talent. In this way many parents would have an opportunity to contribute in a practical way to the Religious Education activity.

Further assistance for Religious Education teachers

Religious Education teachers who are experiencing 'burn-out' or particular difficulties with the subject ought to be given the option of taking a break from it. Parents should encourage and support school authorities in this measure as it would be to the ultimate benefit of all concerned: pupils, teachers and parents. One respondent made the following observation in this regard:

'I feel that Religious Education is something one can only teach short-term i.e. ten years, it's personally draining and demanding.'

Also, in order to ensure a continuing supply of qualified personnel, young people should be encouraged to pursue Religious Education teaching as a career. As we have already seen, the situation now is that there is a majority of lay people involved, and this trend is likely to continue given the decline in vocations.

Student's Textbooks

The teachers' version of 'Christian Way' 1.2 and 3 were considered to be 'excellent' or 'good' by the majority of respondents. Conversely, only a minority described the students' texts as 'excellent' or 'good'. Some of the most frequently-cited changes which respondents would like to see in these texts included the need to change the language, to update the material and to make it more relevant to the lives of young people.

It would appear that proper attention to these matters is long overdue given that the respondents' suggestions merely reflect similar recommendations which have issued from a number of sources from the Council of Trent to the present day, including, of course, the *General Catechetical Directory*. There may be a reluctance on the part of those directly involved to change language etc. lest there be a criticism of its being too 'simplistic'. But this must surely be viewed as less important than the ultimate comprehending by our young people of the Christian message.

Spiritual Development

When asked about the impact they would like Religious Education to have on pupils' lives, the response of the largest number of respondents (N=314) was 'to encourage responsibility and personal development.' A further 293 respondents would like Religious Education 'to assist spiritual development', while 274 respondents would hope it would 'promote a Christian way of life.'

In view of these responses and some other findings of this survey, perhaps the time has come (specifically in relation to senior cycle pupils) for Religious Education, both theoretically and practically, to be called, for example, simply 'Spiritual Development.' This might answer some of the needs expressed by pupils in John McKenna's 'National Survey' which was conducted in 1986/87 prior to the introduction of the 'Living Faith Series.' It might also be assigned to young adolescents that Religious Education personnel are prepared to take them where they're 'at', so to speak.

Future Research

Finally, as both teachers' and pupils' surveys have been conducted at this stage, a corresponding research project into the attitudes, experiences, hopes etc. of parents should now be undertaken. In this way, all concerned will be better able to interpret 'the signs of the times.'

Observations of a bishop

✠ *Donal Murray*

When the Religious Education Teachers' Survey was commissioned it was hoped that it would provide indications as to how the work of Religious Education in Ireland could be assisted and improved. It set out to look at the needs of R.E. teachers, at their morale, at the kind of cooperation they receive, at the resources they require.

The results provide a great range and variety of information. It will take much reflection to tease out the implications; it will need considerable effort and cooperation to ensure that the best use is made of what the Survey tells us.

Different readers of the report will, no doubt, draw different lessons and focus on different aspects. I was most struck by two responses on which the teachers were virtually unanimous.

1) Less than 1% of the respondents disagreed with the statement that, 'A teacher's own faith is a vital component in fostering faith in the classroom.'

2) Over 90% of the respondents believed that, apart from the school situation, there are other effective ways of communicating the Christian message.

This reflects an understanding of Religious Education, which corresponds closely to what is represented in *Catechesi Tradendae*.

In catechesis, it is Christ who teaches and Christ is the Truth who is taught. It is not a matter of communicating dead and abstract truths but of enabling faith to mature and knowledge of God's truth to grow: 'It is the communication of the living mystery of God' (CT 7). Christ is the Teacher, 'Only in deep communion with him will catechists find light and strength for an authentic, desirable renewal of catechesis' (CT 9).

This means that, after the example of Christ the Teacher, a Religious Educator tries to communicate not just in words but in a manner of life, not from an ivory tower but from within the concerns of those who are taught and speaking their language. 'Communication is more than an expression of idea and an indication of emotion. At its most profound level, it is the giving of self in love' (*Communio et Progressio* [1971] 11).

When teachers say that their work is vitally dependent on their own faith, they are indicating a healthy but very demanding understanding of their role. They are also raising questions for the whole community of the Church.

How can we help this faith, which is 'a vital component' of the work of Religious Education, to be nourished and deepened? It would be interesting to know what extent, if any, the impressive commitment to in-service courses is an expression of this need - and how far these courses meet the need; it would be interesting to know whether the opportunities to discuss R.E. with other Religion teachers are generally thought to be adequate. One wonders how serious a problem it is that 15% of respondents say that they have no such opportunities at all. What kind of supports are provided to sustain and strengthen the faith of Religious Educators? How adequate and how accessible are these supports?

The clear awareness that the work of the teacher is one among many ways of communicating the message is also very much in harmony with *Catechesi Tradendae*. The whole community has a two-fold responsibility for the education of its members in faith:

'It has the responsibility of providing for the training of its members, but it also has the responsibility of welcoming them into an environment where they can live as fully as possible what they have learned' (CT 24)

On reading the report one sees that a great deal of effort and considerable resources have been put into the first part of that responsibility. This is not to suggest that there is any reason for complacency and, indeed, the call for increased effort and further resources is clear in the survey results.

On the other hand, I find in the survey strong reinforcement of what has been a growing conviction for many years: that the second element of that responsibility requires particular attention. The most urgent question of all is about the living community of faith which is meant to receive the person being catechised. If this does not happen as it should, 'catechesis runs the risk of becoming barren' (CT 24)

This sense of belonging to an identifiable community may be part of the explanation of the high profile of Religious Education in schools in the North of Ireland. It does, however, make even more unexpected the apparently low profile of R.E. in rural and small town schools, especially among senior pupils. Whatever the reason for this response, it is evident that Religious Educators consistently and rightly reject the idea that education in faith can be left to the school alone.

Almost 90% of the respondents would, for example, like to see cooperation between school and parish in teaching RE. Of the 10% or so who would not, more than half explain that they believe that this would not be realistically possible.

This survey, and the discussions arising from it could bear rich fruit and do much to diminish the risk of barrenness. What is required is a widespread reflection as to how we could make more effective the process by which the larger 'community of faith and Christian life takes in the catechumen at a certain stage of his or her catechesis' (CT 24. It is a reflection which will need to involve all the various areas listed in responses to the question about 'other effective ways of getting across the Christian message'. These would include homes, parishes, clubs, retreats, prayer meetings, media, folk group, social work and so on. It is a challenge to all the members of the Church in all the areas of life in which they are found.

In particular, this involves the role of the home and of the parish.

In a world where pressures and difficulties are continually present, we need, as a pastoral priority to give heart to Christian families. In them takes place the catechesis which precedes, accompanies and enriches all other forms of catechesis (CT 68):

'In the storm in which it finds itself, called as it is into question, the Christian family is more and more often tested by despondency, by lack of confidence in itself and by fear. We need, however, to say to the family with truth and conviction, that it has a mission and a place in the world of today and that for fulfilling that task it bears within itself formidable resources and imperishable values' (Pope John Paul II, 12 October 1980).

The danger of leaving Religious Education to the school alone poses a particular challenge to parishes. The fact that, especially in urban areas, teenagers often attend schools far removed from their parish, raises the urgent question: how can these young people be received into the community of the parish and invited to see themselves as vital elements in its life? In what sense are such young people seen as parishioners by themselves, by the clergy, by the community in general? If things are not as we would wish them to be in this area, the consequences for education in faith must be serious because 'the parish community must continue to be the prime mover and the pre-eminent place for catechesis' (CT 67).

For this reason, it would be a great pity if this report were thought to be of interest only to schools and to Religious Educators. It should, rather, serve to remind all of us that 'catechesis always had been and always will be a work for which the whole Church must feel responsible and must wish to be responsible' (CT 16).

CONTRIBUTORS

Sean Cahill is a Diocesan Advisor and priest of Down and Connor Diocese.

Elizabeth Cotter is a Loreto Sister and Principal of Loreto College, St Stephen's Green, Dublin 2.

Ann M. Hanley is a Research Assistant of the Council for Research and Development at St Patrick's College, Maynooth, Co. Kildare.

Dermot A. Lane is a priest of the Dublin Diocese and Director of Studies at Mater Dei Institute of Education, Clonliffe Road, Dublin 3.

Anne Looney is a qualified catechist teaching at Assumption Secondary School, Walkinstown, Dublin 12.

Cóirle McCarthy is a Mercy Sister and Diocesan Advisor in Cork.

Brian Mooney is a teacher working in Oatlands C.B.S., Mount Merrion, Co. Dublin.

✠ **Donal Murray** is Chairman of the Episcopal Catechetics Commission and Auxiliary Bishop of Dublin.

Siobhan Riordan is a parent and teacher in South Presentation Secondary School, Cork.

John A. Weafer is Director of the Council for Research and Development at St Patrick's College, Maynooth, Co. Kildare.